THOMAS BERNHARD AND HIS GRANDFATHER

JOHANNES FREUMBICHLER

Studies in Austrian Literature, Culture and Thought

Caroline Markolin

THOMAS BERNHARD AND HIS GRANDFATHER JOHANNES FREUMBICHLER:

"OUR GRANDFATHERS ARE OUR TEACHERS"

Translated by
Petra Hartweg

Afterword by
Erich Wolfgang Skwara

ARIADNE PRESS

Translated from the German *Die Großväter sind die Lehrer.*
Johannes Freumbichler und sein Enkel Thomas Bernhard,
©1988 Otto Müller Verlag, Salzburg.

Library of Congress Cataloging-in-Publication Data

Markolin, Caroline, 1957-
    [Grossväter sind Lehrer. English]
    Thomas Bernhard and his grandfather Johannes Freumbichler:
our grandfathers are our teachers / Caroline Markolin ; translated by
Petra Hartweg ; preface by Erich Wolfgang Skwara.
        p.   cm. -- (Studies in Austrian literature, culture, and
thought.)
    ISBN 0-929497-51-1
    1. Freumbichler, Johannes, 1881-1949--Biography.
2. Bernhard, Thomas--Biography. 3. Authors, Austrian--20th
century--Biography.
I. Title. II Series.
PT2611.R473Z7813 1993
838'.91409--dc20   92-38175
[B]   CIP

Cover Design:
Art Director & Designer: George McGinnis

26852551

Contents

Abbreviations

U = Thomas Bernhard, *Die Ursache. Eine Andeutung.*
Salzburg: Residenz, 1975.

Ke= Thomas Bernhard, *Der Keller. Eine Entziehung.*
Salzburg: Residenz, 1976.

A = Thomas Bernhard, *Der Atem. Eine Entscheidung.*
Salzburg: Residenz, 1978.

Ki= Thomas Bernhard, *Ein Kind.* Salzburg: Residenz,
1982.

Preface

What does the reader associate with the name Johannes Freumbichler? Is he a regional writer of the time between the two world wars who was awarded the Austrian State Prize in 1937? Or does one think of the "grandfather" in Thomas Bernhard's autobiography?

Freumbichler's works have been preserved in the Salzburg literary archives; they comprise unpublished manuscripts and numerous diaries as well as his extensive correspondence; the addressees are friends and relatives. From their viewpoint we are allowed a closer look at the writer and the private person of Johannes Freumbichler.

On reading the profusion of postcards and letters an eventful and moving life unfolds, a life so unique in itself that any attempt at rigid classification is rendered futile.

With my picture of Johannes Freumbichler's life I would like to present the correspondence in a coherent manner and to pass on the essence of these letters without any interpretation; I also refrain from attributing any judgements or assumptions.

Whatever might seem incomplete is due to the fact that it was not mentioned in the letters. Moreover, this biography does not reflect the intellectual mood of the time. Johannes Freumbichler lived and worked in isolation from society. He showed love for only a few persons.

The closeness to his grandchild is manifested in Thomas Bernhard's autobiography. Excerpts from these memoirs will accompany Johannes Freumbichler's life story in the following. Mr. Fabjan's kind contributions have helped make this life portrait public. I would like to thank him for supplying the photographs and his assistance in the completion of this book.

Salzburg, October 1987
Caroline Markolin

Johannes Freumbichler

Johannes Freumbichler was born on October 22, 1881 in Henndorf on the Wallersee.

The area had always been the home of his ancestors. His father, Josef Freumbichler (born March 14, 1830) came from the town of Michaelbeuern. For nine years he served as an artilleryman at Cattaro, an Austrian military seaport at that time. Later he worked for the railway company until he and his wife Maria Freumbichler, née

2

Joseph Freumbichler

Langer (born in 1850), moved to Henndorf to live in the so-called "Binderhaus." Johannes Freumbichler's mother was a farmer's daughter from Eling, a village not far from Henndorf. Josef Freumbichler had opened a grocery

Maria Freumbichler

store in Henndorf and had succeeded in expanding his business; his butter was sold as far away as Vienna.

Johannes Freumbichler showed no interest in becoming a grocer. After completing elementary school in Henndorf he wanted to enter college in Salzburg.

The grandfathers are the teachers, the true philosophers of every human being; they pull back the curtain which others continuously try to close. When we are with them, we can see what is real, we see not just the audience, we see the stage, and we see everything behind the stage. For thousands of years the grandfathers have created the devil where, without them, only God would reign. Through grandfathers we comprehend the full scenario, not just the pathetic and hypocritical farce making up the rest. Grandfathers turn the grandchild's head at least to things of interest, though not always of elementary importance, and through their persistant attention we find release from the drab wretchedness which, were it not for grandfathers, would doubtlessly soon choke us. My grandfather on my mother's side rescued me from the dullness and the dreary stench of this earthly tragedy which has already suffocated billions and billions. (Ki 27/28)

"It was a beautiful spring day, everywhere trees, fountains and farmers working their fields and giving candid greetings. Despite all this I found myself in a melancholic mood: I strolled, together with my singing and frolicking grandchild, on a path that reverberated with the thrills and the secrets of my own childhood. I have wandered this way at the most different of times, in the most different of conditions but there were always two bright stars shining down on me . . . and these stars were: father and mother . . ." (Johannes Freumbichler, Good Friday 1936)

My grandfather came from a family of farmers, grocers and innkeepers, and his father had taken up the arduous task of writing only at the age of twenty and had written a letter to his father from the fort Cattaro, a letter which he claimed to have written himself—a statement my grandfather would always dispute. The decades spent on serving beer and examining the butter brought by the farmers on their bicycles and the continuous speculating with property and buildings had roused his suspicion in very early years. Buying and selling ultimately led to nothing else but a mere accumulation of fortunes, and already at the age of twenty he had renounced everything that was to be in store for him. (Ki 46)

But all I want to say is that the business tradition in our family is a very old one; Aunt Rosina's father, my grandfather's father and thus my great-grandfather, was, as can still be read on the tombstone in Henndorf, a so-called wholesaler. He would deliver butter and lard from the Flachgau farmers to the Vienna "Naschmarkt"—an activity that earned him not only the name "Schmalz-sepp," and fame all over the Flachgau, but also a considerable fortune. To this day, many people in the Flachgau area still remember who is meant by "Schmalz-sepp" and this name commands highest respect when they ask me who I am and where I come from. (Ke 129)

At first he was supposed to be butter wholesaler, innkeeper, property speculator like his father, after his older brother had been lost to the profession of forest warden. (Ki 55)

6

SALZBURG

In 1895 Johannes Freumbichler began his studies at a boarding school located in the Schrannengasse where he lived until September 1901. In the fall of 1901 he moved to Gstättengasse, Stieglbräukeller, and for the months of February and March 1902 he rented a room at Späthgasse 8, Riedenburg.

Whenever she could, his mother sent food and money. After school hours Freumbichler worked in the Stieglbräukeller restaurant. He stayed in contact with his family through his older brother Rudolf (born in 1874), with whom he shared common ground in many ways.

His parents' business did not appeal to Rudolf either. In a letter dated September 31, 1901 he wrote to his brother: "I will now try everything in my power to leave Henndorf, the time has come, I must go, for I am in distress . . . What I have endured all day, no one will know, nobody will understand but those who suffer from the same kind of nervousness. And to make it worse, I have this insurmountable fear . . . How often I have cringed today, a hundred times, when the door opened, when again somebody came with butter; how I suffered when I had to talk to these people, when I hear a child cry, it is terrible" (1901/1).* On learning that a twenty-two-year-old teacher from Henndorf had committed suicide he stated: "What he has done, I will do, only the

---

*The letter number given in parentheses corresponds to the catalogue system which the author set up in the Salzburg Literary Archives.

*My grandfather had been deeply deceived and disap-
pointed by his relatives from Salzburg; they had cheated
him in every way and had brought great misery upon him
when he had thought he could turn to them for help,
instead of supporting him at the time of his own young
helplessness as a student. (U 60)*

Rudolf Freumbichler applied for employment as a forest warden near Salzburg, but his efforts were in vain, and the continuous rejections made him even more restless and depressed. On December 29, 1901, he traveled to Vienna where his sister Marie (born March 25, 1875) lived with her husband Ferdinand Russ (born June 17, 1872) and their two children, Fernanda and Roland. Like her brothers Johannes and Rudolf, Marie had not wanted to stay in Henndorf. Her husband, Ferdinand Russ, also from Henndorf, was never liked by her family due to his constant debts (1903/5). For this reason Marie moved with Ferdinand to Vienna where she opened a business.

Ferdinand Russ, a painter, also worked as a restorer for an art dealer (1901/8). His sister had been Johannes Freumbichler's girlfriend when he still lived at home in Henndorf (1902/17).

In January 1902 Rudolf Freumbichler tried, once again, to find work as a forest warden in the country. For the time being he earned his living shoveling snow (1902/18). When he was without luck again that month, he and the Russ family moved to Mollardgasse 14/2/13, Vienna VI. Marie meanwhile had had to give up the business and was looking for work as well. From a letter to Johannes Freumbichler we learn that every day four to five hundred unemployed "suffering from misery, hunger and sorrow" (1902/15) would gather at the Schulerstraße to wait for the latest newspaper editions. Marie Russ succeeded in running her own business by obtaining a license for a soup kitchen where she cooked daily for about fifteen people (1902/16).

In the weeks to follow, Rudolf Freumbichler's attempts to obtain work as a forest warden failed again (1902/17). He was discouraged because only "protegés"

His older sister Marie had also recognized this stupid routine as an unreasonable demand on her, and had, at a young age, married a so-called painter from Eger who later became a celebrity in Mexico. (Ki 46)

An older brother of my grandfather, Rudolf, had sought refuge in the forest, and as a warden of the Duke's woods around the Wallersee and the Mondsee he committed suicide at the age of thirty-two. At least, because he "could no longer bear the misery of the world," as one could read on the handwritten note found next to his corpse and beside the dachshund guarding the corpse. (Ki 47/48)

(1902/18) found work. Disappointed with the "great and the rich" he wrote to Johannes Freumbichler on February 4, 1902, conveying his communist views: "To have a home, to be loved, is an impossible goal for the poor, the rich will always push aside the common worker; oh dogs, horses, parrots, etc., you are to be envied being with the rich! Oh you rich rotten souls, how you treat human beings! Aren't they worth more than animals? The servant is not a member of your family, but a necessary evil that you employ to torture" (1902/18).

In his growing hatred he saw his last hope in his brother Johannes, with whom he wanted to win the struggle for freedom. On February 4, 1902 he wrote: "Dear Brother, let us go to the forests of Bohemia—no, to Italy where it is warm, up into the mountains if you want to be free.—Free until death comes." Or: "Let us die together, we will never leave each other, humans are bad, and so are the women . . . Only he who strives to carry out his ideas is a man, only he who knows how to die . . . If you don't agree, our ways shall lead us apart, farewell!" (1902/18).

On March 7, 1902 Rudolf Freumbichler took his life.

In Salzburg, Johannes Freumbichler befriended a girl from Mattighofen by the name of Cilli Reitsperger, who lived with the family for whom she was working as a maid (1901/6). During the vacations that Johannes Freumbichler spent with his parents in Henndorf he sent her numerous letters and poems (1901/5). On the very day of his brother's suicide, she received a telegram with the sad news. From this moment on, Cilli Reitsperger was in doubt, and she responded immediately: "Tell me, dear Hans, you don't want to scare me, for you used to have similar ideas in the past. Only the thought of your beloved mother held you back. I can't

11

Rudolf Freumbichler

According to my grandfather his brother, the forest warden, of whom I possess several photographs, shot himself with his gun at the highest point on the Zifanken and left a note at the site of his death, giving as the reason for shooting himself that he "could no longer bear the misery of the world." (Ke 127/128)

help thinking that you don't like me at all, for otherwise you could not have the heart to do such a thing" (1902/21). Under the influence of her parents and fearful of a possible suicide, Cilli Reitsperger decided to break off with him: "When my parents learned of your brother's tragic death and then of your letter proclaiming him as a hero . . . they warned me of continuing our relationship. I was very upset because you mentioned more than once that you would . . . And I could not bear the embarrassment of seeing that happen to you" (1902/22).

During his years at high school, Johannes Freumbichler joined a fraternity, the "Iron Circle" (CH = Cheruskia), whose members shared the idea of freedom, demonstrated by one of their mottos: "We, the brothers of the alliance, we want to do as Schiller says: Let's face the rough world. Let's work and strive to make our luck" (1902/45). Among the "brothers" mentioned in the letters are Sieghart, Rüdiger, Tuisko and Gieselher. Freumbichler's *nom de guerre* was "Werinhard." His friend Gieselher's real name is Rudolf Kasparek.

Kasparek was born on March 29, 1884 in Graz. His mother had died young (March 29, 1893). When his father, who lived with the children in Hallein, had lost his second wife, he was "physically and mentally broken" (1902/34) and, due to the "wretchedness of people" (ibid.), he felt too weak to look after himself and his children. As a consequence, the oldest son Rudolf assumed responsibility for the family.

The family situation weighed heavily on him. More and more he felt the need for his friend; yet he knew that he himself would always be there for Johannes Freumbichler. At the height of the crisis with Cilli Reitsperger Kasparek advised him to turn to "the love of

13

. . . that it was man's most precious gift to renounce the world voluntarily through suicide, to kill oneself whenever one thought it convenient. He himself had played with this idea throughout his entire life, this was his most passionate speculation, I have adopted it for myself. Anytime, whenever we want to, he said, we can commit suicide, in the best of taste if possible, he said. Indeed, to run off, he said, was the only truly wonderful thought. (Ki 30).

In Salzburg he acquired the taste for it: "Schopenhauer, Nietzsche, I had no idea that something like this existed," he said. (Ki 56)

My grandfather's younger sister Rosina had stayed at home, a true, genuine child of the idyllic world, unable to travel even ten kilometers away from Henndorf, Rosina who had never in her life been to Vienna, probably not even to Salzburg, whom I admired at the age of three or four and much later as the empress of her buy-and-sell emporium. (Ki 47)

All of them, except Rosina, were fugitives, had had enough of the idle and monotonous routine of rural life. (Ki 48)

The grocery milieu was not new to me; my grandfather's sister, Rosina, ran a grocery store in her parents' house in Henndorf, and some of the high points of my childhood consisted of being with my great-aunt in the store while she served her customers. (Ke 126/127)

14

brothers and friends" (1902/26); he himself had found comfort in friendship after a disappointing relationship with a woman. He reminisced: "You certainly remember the day when I came to see you, confused and in tears, nearly heartbroken, when I urged you to go with me, regardless of what might happen" (1902/34).

ALTENBURG

In April 1902 Johannes Freumbichler moved to Altenburg in Saxony for technical schooling. He stayed at Karlstraße 6/2. His mother supplied him with a monthly allowance of thirty florins (in comparison: Marie paid one hundred twenty florins for her flat in Vienna every three months [1902/12]). In every letter she admonished him to save as much as he could, since the butter and lard trade did not yield enough money. Saving money to her meant: no beer, not too many books and no bad company, for it only caused distress (1902/5-14). Sometimes his younger sister Rosina sent money behind their mother's back.

Rosina Freumbichler (born February 27, 1878) assisted her mother in running the grocery store and a boarding house. In 1902, Rosina already had a seven-year-old son, Sebastian (born December 29, 1894); in 1909 she married Josef Schlager.

In Altenburg Johannes Freumbichler made the acquaintance of Hans Sedletzky. With him he could talk about literature, and Sedletzky recommended that he read Sienkiewicz's *Quo vadis* and Spielhagen's *Born Free* (not dated, to JF/2). Writing poems for the "Iron Circle," Freumbichler kept in contact with Salzburg (1902/41).

Rudolf Kasparek felt very lonely without his friend (1902/31). Numerous letters were to substitute for their conversations about freedom, art, and life. However, the separation would reinforce the relationship to such an extent that Kasparek's feelings for Johannes Freumbichler seemed to go beyond those of mere friendship. He wrote to him: "The feelings I harbor for you I cannot explain. Should I ever be given a chance to be happy again, I will owe everything that is noble and beautiful to you. You rekindled feelings in me that I thought would be lost forever, for I doubted almost everything. It is gratefulness I feel, it is affection, friendship and yet all these together. Maybe you understand, maybe you don't, but it is a kind of love I feel for you. Could I only be with you, I know I could easily abandon the love of a woman" (1902/24).

Freumbichler shared these feelings. The poems he wrote for his friend attributed "absolute beauty" to him (1902/32). During this period both read books on homosexual love. At the same time they encouraged each other in their ideals of freedom. Kasparek: "Let us be idealists, you write, but we do not wait merely looking on, no, we want to dedicate all our strength to make the ideal dreams that fill our young hearts come true" (1902/43).

Next to freedom, love held the highest value. Love that embraced the world, love as the origin of life. "Love has built this world," according to Kasparek (1902/33). Whenever he encouraged Freumbichler he would say: ". . . there is still one hope—love" (1902/23). With a father unable to work, Kasparek lived under the poorest of conditions, but nevertheless he said: "Do I need riches? No! There is a more precious treasure . . . I have you, and I need nothing but a true and

. . . *my grandmother, she had often and time and again told me about her dreadful childhood and youth in this nothing but dreadful town and among these cold people who were her relatives. She had had anything but a pleasant childhood, so it was obvious that she—after she had been at the age of seventeen married by her parents, a couple of wholesalers, to a wealthy Salzburg master tailor of forty—would break out of this marriage, which had given her three children, and go to Basel to follow my grandfather. She had met him while looking from her flat onto the Priesterhaus on Priesterhausgasse—to accompany him, who was not an easy man to live with, for the rest of her life. She had left her children behind only to get away from this hated, always incredibly cruel man, at the young age of twenty-one. This is why she broke out from this marriage that had been nothing but a business deal. (U 133)*

loving soul!" (1902/30).

In November 1902 the Kasparek family lost everything to an impostor (1902/37). Kasparek merely shrugged it off, for he comprehended: "Life is not a dream, life is an eternal rude awakening" (1902/39).

Possessing a deep love for life, he proclaimed in response to Johannes Freumbichler's repeated thoughts of committing suicide: "And now to your last will. Listen, what on earth was going through your mind then? To die—what nonsense. You and I, we will live for a long time yet! What a joyous thought to have!" (1902/41).

Like Freumbichler, Kasparek also wrote poems. Very early, however, he saw the greater talent in his friend: "You, my dear friend, believe me, you possess a godly gift. Today I implore you to never refrain from expressing your deepest sentiments which will be the greatest gift for posterity" (1902/43).

Kasparek kept Freumbichler up to date on the other members of the fraternity. Tuisko lived in Salzburg, renting a room from a Mrs. Anna Bernhard (born June 20, 1878, née Schönberg). Her husband, Karl Bernhard, was a tailor. They had two children. Mrs. Bernhard, however, had not found fulfillment in her marriage. She fell in love with Kasparek, who often came to see Tuisko. Kasparek could not respond to these feelings. In November 1902, he conveyed his deep compassion for the young woman to Freumbichler: "She is a good and noble creature, still a child, so innocent and pure. In tears she has told me all about her grief. Almost a child still, she, who had always been neglected, was joined with this man she thought she loved . . . In short, at the age of seventeen and without the faintest idea of those endless, horrible obligations she got married. She became

a mother, was happy about her child—and her husband? He never ever had a loving word for her, let alone a gift. He does not even allow her to read!" (1902/40).

Kasparek did not want to abandon the "poor and innocent thing" (ibid.). Together with Tuisko he devised plans to help Anna Bernhard.

ILMENAU

In March 1903, Johannes Freumbichler moved to Ilmenau in Thuringia to attend courses at a school for electrotechnology. From mid-March to June 1903 he stayed at Alexanderstraße 23. In the summer months he lived at Am Zeihenhaus 9/1, and from September 1903 to the end of the year at Marienstraße 14/2.

In January 1903 Rudolf Kasparek had been expelled from high school in Salzburg: it was not considered "proper" for a student to take his meals at inns and to have a room with a separate entrance (1903/25). Since his father was unable to keep an eye on him in Salzburg and since boarding school was too costly, Kasparek returned to his family in Hallein. At this point he did not know what would become of him; he did not have enough money for the technical school in Steyr which he had thought of attending. Kasparek asked Johannes Freumbichler to advise him on his "future career" (1903/29). Freumbichler suggested that he move to Ilmenau and attend the technical school there. Kasparek was enthusiastic about this idea; but the imminent prospect of seeing his friend so close and not being able to join him right away, made him feel restless: "I owe it to me and to you not to say yes to suggestions which

21

might prove uncertain, yes, even impossible . . . If I give you a definite yes now, I will be utterly distressed if one day I am faced with the possibility of not seeing you at all" (1902/32).

After a lot of deliberating Kasparek made up his mind: "For once I will have to see whether I possess enough moral strength to realize the dreams that brought me many blissful nights" (1903/31). His discussions with Freumbichler about freedom were not to be just empty words, and he wanted do everything in his power to realize these thoughts: "I no longer fear the twists of fate, I will stand up to them, be strong and undaunted, firm and courageous! Come what may, I am sick of protecting myself from dangers. It is quite the contrary I am after. I will challenge life wherever I can!" (1903/31).

On March 14, 1903, Kasparek requested an enrollment form for the technical school in Ilmenau. His father turned a deaf ear to his son's plans. However, on seeing his son's "displeasure and bitterness" (1903/37), he forwarded the application himself in the hope of receiving a rejection.

On April 13, 1903, Johannes Freumbichler received a telegram with the message: "Arrival tomorrow at 10:18. Kasparek" (1903/35). Rudolf Kasparek moved in with Freumbichler at Alexanderstraße. Their dream of living and learning together, of enjoying stimulating conversations and of writing together, was fulfilled.

From Ilmenau Kasparek stayed in contact with Tuisko and Mrs. Bernhard. Through the intervention of Kasparek, Freumbichler wrote to her on September 9, 1903: "Dear Mrs. Bernhard! . . . Honored by your trust in me, I have long felt the desire to write . . . I do not know you nor your appearance . . . I have never seen you al-

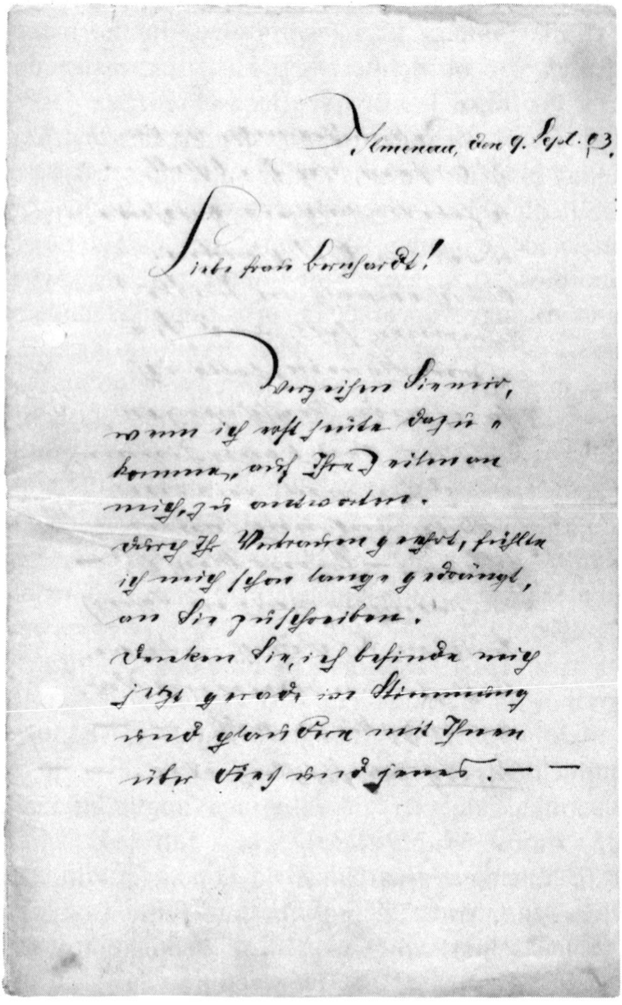

Ilmenau, den 9. Sept. 03.

Liebe Frau Bernhardt!

Verzeihen Sie mir, wenn ich erst heute dazu komme, auf Ihre Zeilen an mich zu antworten. Durch Ihr Vertrauen geehrt, fühlte ich mich schon lange gedrängt, an Sie zu schreiben. Denken Sie, ich befinde mich jetzt gerade in Stimmung und plaudere mit Ihnen über Dies und Jenes. — —

Johannes Freumbichler to Anna Bernhard (9 September 1903)

though you believe that I did because I was sitting in Tuisko's room when you entered. Yet the most violent of headaches seized me and caused the entire room and you with it to turn like a whirlwind. In the month of November you came into my life . . . like a comet . . . into the world of my imagination" (1903/39).

Freumbichler also sent her poems. When she asked for their meaning he responded: "Poems never mean anything. Poems are just poems" (ibid.). Mrs. Bernhard described her unhappy marriage to Freumbichler as well. According to him, there was no other solution but the "liberation from slavery." In passionate terms he proclaimed vividly: "More liberated creatures, more noble human beings stand up against such a disgraceful and humiliating treatment, stand up against the violation of human dignity and demand their rights and their freedom. A great movement has been formed, the emancipation or liberation of women with the goal of giving back to women their freedom and welfare . . . Dear Mrs. Bernhard! The sun of a new era is shining. We are on the threshold of a new world which will sweep away all pain and sorrow!" (1903/39). Freumbichler's attitude was supported even more strongly by his life with Kasparek: "I and Rudl, we live a happy and merry life together despite all the sorrows we have—and there are more than enough. We love each other and laugh at the world! Laugh with us!" (1903/39). They solemnly admitted Anna Bernhard to their idealist alliance: "With a hand on your heart, swear the holy oath of faith! Live on this sacred friendship! One thought is flashing through us! One love is living in us! One happiness is in all of us! Bear for now what is inevitable. Or . . . ? The day will come when happiness will embrace you. Have hope! Think of me! . . . We are the prophets of a new era.

25

My grandfather loved the extraordinary and the uncommon, the contradictory, the revolutionary, he thrived on contradiction, his whole existence was based on conflict. (Ki 43)

We do not talk to the rabble, but to friends and brothers of our souls" (1903/39).

Not only did Freumbichler and Kasparek agree on questions of revolution and anarchism, they also shared the same view on women. Kasparek: "Well, you know what I think about women. Every woman who acts like an inflated and terribly emancipated creature in this 'world of monkeys,' who still clings doggedly to the bone that is called 'fashion,' has lost the right to call herself a woman . . . Their eyes flicker with stupidity, their speeches proclaim the bright spirit of 'civilization.' But there are also other women!" (1903/33). Anna Bernhard was one of them.

When Kasparek left Salzburg, Anna Bernhard directed all her dreams and desires towards Tuisko. In September 1903, she wrote to Johannes Freumbichler: "The more I got to know Tuisko, the more I listened to his words, the clearer it became to me that he is the one without whom I cannot live" (AB-JF/1). Unfortunately, Tuisko did not share these feelings, and she was bewildered when he told her that he was certainly in love with her but it was "not an ideal love" (ibid.).

As a consequence, she wanted to leave for Ilmenau to see her friends: ". . . do allow me to be with you. I would find ways to support myself . . . Any day now I expect my husband to throw me out" (ibid.).

Anna Bernhard still would have to wait. She was invited to a reunion of the members of the "Iron Circle" which was arranged for Christmas 1903 in Salzburg. In September she wrote to Freumbichler: "To come for Christmas, how beautiful that sounds, I may see you, may talk to you, may shake your hand . . . Help me to gain my freedom. I urge you from the bottom of my heart" (AB-JF/2).

Then, on October 17, 1903: "Oh you, how I rejoice at the thought of you and Rudolf, of you coming to Salzburg. It is this hope that keeps me going" (AB-JF/3).

At the end of October 1903: "Oh, if the time I am longing for had already come, how comfortable I could make everything for you . . . oh you, I am overjoyed at the thought alone. When you come at Christmas, you will have to decide whether you want to have me with you. It is hard to wait" (AB-JF/4).

And in the following letter: "If only Christmas was here soon . . . Although I cannot shake off this fear in me, and I wonder why? . . . Well, we will see. Everything is only up to you!" (AB-JF/5).

And at the beginning of November: "I am waiting patiently, I know it will not be forever . . . one day I will pack up and come to you . . ." (AB-JF/8).

BASEL

Johannes Freumbichler chose a life with Anna Bernhard. He and "Dietlinde" left Ilmenau and moved to Basel at the beginning of 1904. Until April 1904 they stayed at Hegenheimerstraße 12/2, and from May 1904 to the fall of 1905 at Gasstraße 33/3.

Kasparek returned to Hallein. But already one month later, on February 1, 1904, he wrote to Johannes Freumbichler: "I will soon come to Basel, for here nothing is to be found but fear and pain! It is there that I would like to work and live, and if my feeling is right, achieve greatness" (1904/10). He intended to study chemistry in Basel. Like Freumbichler, he was full of enthusiasm over a new beginning. "I too carry the flame of strength and

. . . Switzerland where he studied technology and socialized with a few anarchists with similar interests. It was the time of Lenin and Kropotkin. He had not gone to Zurich, but to Basel and let his hair grow long. Some old pictures show him with frayed pants, and on his nose he sported the famous and notorious anarchist's pince-nez. However, he did not dedicate his energies to politics but to literature. He lived next to the house of the famous Lou Salomé. Every month his sister Rosina would send him a box with butter and sausages. His companion through life, my grandmother, who had lived through a terrifying marriage with a Salzburg master tailor forced upon her by her parents, appeared in Basel, leaving husband and two children behind, flung her arms around my grandfather's neck and pleaded to stay with him forever from now on, no matter where. (Ki 48/49)

energy in me . . . let us march on, without a rest, let us march on in the storm toward a brighter world" (ibid.). Everything had been arranged for his departure, but familial and financial obstacles still stood in the way of his "desire to leave everything behind" (ibid.).

For Freumbichler, Basel marked the beginning of numerous problems. He attended technical school, but he lacked the money to provide for himself and Dietlinde. Once again his mother was forced to help. She, in turn, only wanted to support her son, and was not interested in his involvement with "this woman." Although she knew that Anna Bernhard was expecting a child, she wrote to her son: ". . . try to get rid of her. She will do again what she did to her husband who took care of her: she deceived him. What am I supposed to think of a woman who leaves two beautiful children behind—she is a terrible mother. The same thing will happen to you; once she has the child she will forget you for another man, this miserable woman . . . Chase her away, you'd rather pay if there is a child and you will be free. This woman will not set foot into my house; for you I will do everything . . ." (1904/6).

In response to a similar remark by his mother on March 1904 Freumbichler evoked terms like "contempt for human beings" and "hatred" in a letter to Kasparek. Kasparek's answer formed the counterbalance to Maria Freumbichler's attitude: "Tell Dietlinde that I greet her sincerely, with all my heart, tell her that I hold her in high esteem, that I respect her and love her, for I see in her the first free woman without fear" (1904/12).

Kasparek could only offer moral support. He had to live under dreadful conditions. For days he and his family had to go without food. He reproached his father for not being able to provide for his children. "Is it

. . . and he had broken loose, something unheard of at that time, just before the turn of the century, to go to Basel in order to lead the dangerous life of an anarchist like Kropotkin, and later he had been, together with his wife, my grandmother, an anarchist living under the most dreadful of conditions, always wanted by the authorities and often caught and imprisoned. In 1904 my mother was born in Basel . . . (U 130)

cowardice or disease? I do not know" (1904/3). Three months had passed, and Kasparek had no means to leave Hallein. Freumbichler saw no way of living any longer in Basel. He would have liked to go to Henndorf, but this was not feasible. His mother did not want the neighbors to see that he was still with Dietlinde. He was supposed to stay in Basel and not mention her in his letters. On July 28, 1904 she wrote: "don't say anything about this woman" (1904/7).

With greatest difficulty Kasparek managed to leave for Basel. In July 1904, he reached Zürich where he had to find work to earn enough money to continue his journey. He obtained temporary employment with a doctor. He stayed in Zürich for at least a month (1904/14). The correspondence does not show whether he ever made it to Basel. In December of 1904, Freumbichler received news from Kasparek from Lauterbach near Bregenz that he was working as an office clerk in a factory (1904/17). He intended to travel to Meran to cure his ill lungs at the beginning of the following year: "This is where the third chapter of my life will begin" (ibid.).

The same letter of December 19, 1904 reveals that Freumbichler was very unhappy: "It can hardly get worse for you. I urge you, carry on! You will win! What you have lost and what you have suffered I can only imagine" (ibid.). Despite his difficult situation, Freumbichler started a literary work in Basel. Kasparek saw this as the only hope: "Peace will come" (ibid.).

On December 21, 1904, Anna Bernhard gave birth in Basel to a daughter by the name of Hertha. The name had been chosen by their mutual friend Rudolf Kasparek; in brief words he had written one week before the child was born: "I choose: Farald or Hertha" (1904/16).

Rudolf Kasparek to Johannes Freumbichler (25 December 1904)

On December 25, Kasparek urged Freumbichler again not to give up: "As soon as I can—and I will try everything—I will send you as much as possible. I wrote to Tuisko to forward as much money as possible by cable. Please, be strong!!! The bad times will pass! It grieves me that I cannot be at your side to help you" (1904/18).

In January 1905, Kasparek accepted a position with 'Electrobosna' in Meran. Now he was finally able to help Freumbichler. On March 22, 1905, he sent money and jewelry which he had inherited from his father. He wrote: "By the way, do as you wish with the objects. However, may I ask you to preserve the most precious ones if you can, for my father—a hero—held them in high esteem. If this is impossible, it does not matter to me, for you are the most precious jewel! . . . Be strong!" (1905/2).

In May 1905, Freumbichler decided to leave Basel to see Kasparek in Meran. Anna Bernhard was supposed to follow with their child as soon as suitable living conditions were established. Freumbichler expected the Mediterranean climate to bring relief to his irritated lungs.

Kasparek was in good spirits at the thought of being allowed to reunite with his friend in due course. On August 25, 1905 he wrote: "At last relieved! My dear friend, hurry up! . . . hurry up into the arms of your friend. Don't expect paradise here, but at least you won't have to worry about your daily bread" (1905/6). He also planned to put aside three marks every month to redeem Freumbichler's books from the pawnbroker's.

There was, however, one condition that Kasparek imposed on the reunion: "Not one word ever on what took place between us" (ibid.). The times of youthful

passion were gone, and a precious friendship would be theirs for the future.

MERAN

In the fall of 1905 Freumbichler arrived in Meran. Until September 1906 he lived in Töll. Anna Bernhard and her one-year-old daughter stayed in Salzburg until they were able to join him. On January 15, 1906, Freumbichler started employment as an office clerk with 'Electrobosna,' and on March 9, 1906, he wrote to Dietlinde, asking her to prepare everything for the move: "I feel the urge to tell you that we will live a rather modest life here because our meager financial means will not suffice to operate a decent household. We will have to make sacrifices and renounce many things if we want to be free in a few years" (1906/6). On March 17, 1906 she arrived with Hertha in Meran.

Anna Bernhard wanted to start writing in Meran as well, and she began work on a biography of the friend and poet Rudolf Kasparek. He responded: "Now you are my biographer! This is divine! Has there ever been a more amiable person to do this for a poet? Watch out, my dear, that you don't receive the greater merit for my immortality. I suppose this is sufficient as far as guide-lines go. The rest is up to you" (1909/8).

In October 1906, Freumbichler and his family moved to Partschins near Meran. Kasparek, in the meantime, had left Meran and moved to Munich, Hirschgartenallee 44/3. In mid-February 1907, Freumbichler paid him a visit and stayed until May at Wolfratshauserstraße 31/3, but soon it was time for him to continue his work in Meran. During the same month he moved to Villa

Johannes Freumbichler (1910)

Rosenegg in Lazag. On January 31, 1908 he quit his employment with 'Electrobosna.'

In Munich, Kasparek tried to gain access to publishers, for himself and Freumbichler. He hoped that his contact with Ellen Key would allow him to give his friend a good chance to be published; however, he had misgivings that Freumbichler would not facilitate this: "Most likely she will demand a sample of your writing, and I assume you don't approve of that" (1908/4). In June 1908, Kasparek met a Dr. Ludwig who helped him find work. Because of his recommendation Kasparek was given the opportunity to cooperate with a "philosopher" in a project on Goethe and Hebbel (ibid.).

Kasparek failed to get a publication for Freumbichler; in July 1911, however, Kasparek's first volume of poems was available in print (1911/3).

Freumbichler stayed in Meran until August 1909 to finish a literary work (1908/3, 1909/5).

FORSTENRIED/MUNICH

From September 1909 until May 1911 Johannes Freumbichler lived alternately in Henndorf and Munich. His stay with Kasparek in Munich from February to May 1907 and Kasparek's efforts to establish contacts with publishers had made the city attractive as a future domicile.

On January 19, 1910 Anna Bernhard gave birth to a son, Farald, in Munich. The letters of this period do not indicate any details.

A permanent residence is documented only as of May 1911. Until October 1911, Freumbichler and his family stayed in Forstenried near Munich, where the living

conditions were still poor. Freumbichler's mother again had to support her son with money and food. For his sake she would have even taken care of the children to allow Anna Bernhard to work. On October 2, 1911 Hertha started her first year of school in Forstenried. During the same month Freumbichler moved to Munich, where he lived until the end of the year, staying at Lindenschmidtstraße 29a/4 until February and then at Implerstraße 67/4. Johannes Freumbichler must have left his family behind in Forstenried, for he received letters from Anna Bernhard. Even in Munich Johannes Freumbichler was without work. His financial problems were also known in Salzburg, where he owed a substantial amount to a businessman. Freumbichler could not pay his debts because he had to advance 3,000 marks for the publication (1,500 copies) of a book (1911/2). In October 1911 his novel *Julia Wiedeland* appeared under the C. Huber imprint in Diessen near Munich. Recognizing herself in the novel, Anna Bernhard expressed her delight about the published book: "I read it and I felt once more all my sorrow and joy . . . the time of my marriage, then my children; everything that reminded me of them made me shiver. It seemed to me I was standing at an open grave that robbed me of a great treasure the value of which I realized too late . . . It is here that you show the world a picture of a new marriage" (AB-JF/11).

The novel did not sell too well. On November 22, 1911 Freumbichler wrote to his mother: "It is certainly difficult to get this book going, since the bookstores are filled with cheap trash" (1911/8).

Kasparek, who had lived in Bernried at the Starnberger See since November 1911, helped distribute *Julia* through Mr. Harden in Bernried who was in contact with

Max Dauthendey, Frank Wedekind and Thomas Mann; Rudolf Kasparek expected himself and Freumbichler to benefit substantially from these acquaintances.

Johannes Freumbichler himself was already at work on a new novel (probably *Eduard Aring*) and six novellas (1911/8). His intention was to make a living exclusively at writing. His mother showed understanding: "Every poet has to struggle, and this is true also for you" (1911/6).

In January 1912 Freumbichler changed publishers because Mr. Kleinschmitt of the Huber publishing house charged advances that were beyond his means (1912/1). A new edition was delayed. His mother therefore urged him to find employment "even if it is difficult for you" (1912/2), so as to "finally put an end to this hardship" (ibid.). She also advised him to forward a copy of *Julia Wiedeland* to Gerhart Hauptmann with the request to "consider a loan to save a poet" (1912/9).

From April 1912 to the end of the year Freumbichler took on steady work, but he was dissatisfied with his situation—he wanted to leave for Bozen. His friend Rudolf Kasparek remarked: "I do ask you not to give up yet! In Bozen, you will find work and restore your health" (1912/17).

In the meantime, Kasparek had accomplished a considerable amount of writing. In January 1912, he had submitted four tales to the *Austrian Illustrated Journal* (1912/13): "The Miss" ("Die Miß"), "The First Invitation" ("Die erste Einladung"), "The Tailor in Despair" ("Der Schneider in Verzweiflung") and "The Poor Priest" ("Der arme Pfarrer"). Rudolf Kasparek's poems appeared in an almanac published by Velhagen and Klasing in the fall of 1912 (1912/19).

43

BOZEN

Freumbichler finally moved to Bozen to cure his ill lungs. Munich had not been the city for him to live in: "I suffered terribly in Munich," he writes retrospectively in 1913.

His stay in Bozen was limited to the spring months of 1913, but these few months brought about an important change in Freumbichler's life. In Bozen he met his future patroness, Mrs. Clarita Thomsen.

Mrs. Thomsen (born November 11, 1860) had lived for about twenty-five years with her children in Möltevort, a fishing village close to Kiel. When she had inherited a villa in Gries near Bozen ("Wendtlandhaus"), she had settled down in it (1920/5). In Bozen she devoted herself to literature and painting. She was actively writing. One of her fairy tales, "The Lace Pillow" ("Das Klöppelkissen"), had already been published. Every once in a while she would travel to Munich to see her children, and once a year she spent time at a spa, either in Badgastein, where she stayed at the Elisabethhof, or in Heiligenkreuz in Tyrol.

Johannes Freumbichler finished his novel *Eduard Aring* in Bozen. He began a third novel immediately and also planned to work on a theater play (1913/1). He sent his manuscript of *Eduard Aring* to several publishers, without success. Kasparek, who had moved back to Munich in 1913 (Belgradstraße 159), wanted to show the novel to Albert Langen. On March 29, 1913 he wrote to Freumbichler: "So *Eduard* has not been acknowledged? As a useful book for empty heads? I am not surprised! But never mind, keep sending it out; leave one legible copy for me, I will try to find a publisher. Of course, only on condition that a preprint appears in a magazine,

45

Clarita Thomsen to Anna Bernhard (10 March 1915)

46

which is, as I know, possible without a reduction in royalties. The publisher is Albert Langen. He pays 15% to new authors, however, only as an advance, which amounts to 900 marks for the first print of 2,000 copies. Now, if we could accommodate the novel in a magazine and have a payment of a few thousand, we could very well accept the low rate of 15% for the first edition, especially when keeping in mind that the publications will not rot on the shelves, as is the case with Hans Sachs Publishing" (1913/6).

Two months later Freumbichler learned that Langen had not accepted the novel (1913/8). He also sent several narratives to Kasparek, who moved heaven and earth to find a publisher: "During these two days I have forwarded *Eduard* with high hopes and also tried to accomodate your narratives. As far as they are concerned, regrettably without luck. I will think about it and try to exploit whatever can be exploited. The tales are ready to print and you should by all means try to get them published" (ibid.).

In this crisis Mrs. Thomsen intervened. Despite her own problems she did everything in her power: "I can only help you with the money I have put aside in the bank, there is nothing else at my disposal. You can imagine that this small sum is shrinking considerably due to the expenses for my children and my surroundings. However, I will, for the respective purposes, send you the money this time to do something good and to allow for a better life for you and your wife" (1913/15).

Regarding her support for Johannes Freumbichler, Mrs. Thomsen usually asked the advice of Dr. Weberitsch.

Kasparek as well did not succeed in publishing his literary work. Disturbed by the refusal of one of his novellas by Velhagen he sent his "Meisterstümperwerk"

("masterpiece of botchery") to Freumbichler for a re-vision: "Please be lenient and then tell me the plain truth about it. Maybe then I will continue to write" (1913/8).

Two months later, Kasparek was already working on a series of ballads, "Lady Lilo" (1913/10). Writing, for Kasparek, had an exclusive value: "I am resolved to do nothing else in this world but to write" (1913/9).

In addition to his daily financial problems and the responsibility for his family, Kasparek was plagued by the ever worsening state of his heart and lungs. Very soon he started thinking about his death. he wrote to divert himself from poverty and disease, an attitude he shared with Freumbichler. Writing for him meant to en-courage his friend in times of despair: "My divine friend and brother, if my heart is strong, if there is enough philosophy left in it, I will still create, and if it is only for you, to spare you from a fate of solitude and the loathsomeness of this world. And to elevate you above, to spur you on, that would be my noblest merit. Indeed, comparing myself to you, I may say my mind is not filled with mundane thoughts and my heart is not poor. But—as I told you—it is dying. This is why I produce so little. Last night, I would not dare to fall asleep for fear it was time to make the great unknown journey. Finally I regained my calm: in the morning I got up, and after washing myself I felt content.—To die early, what misery. One must not think about it" (1913/8).

Even in his own hopeless situation, Kasparek still encouraged Freumbichler: "But you, you have to go on writing every day so as not to lose anything of how you experience life. The way you live is unique! I have de-voured the first five tales (I kept "Friedl" for last), I could not help it. I had the most extraordinary experience

49

The wife of the jungle researcher, who owned a majestic, castlelike villa in the most lovely area of Obermais, had my grandmother learn the profession of a midwife. This was to prove valuable later in her life. (Ki 81)

while reading, I had the shivers, and I still haven't found my balance yet. What can I say! In the drab confusion of my pitiful daily sorrows I will hardly be able to add any remarks to each and every of your notebooks. However, I will certainly slip in a little note here and there (1913/8).

He was the only critic for Freumbichler.

SALZBURG/HENNDORF

Freumbichler spent the summer of 1913 in Henndorf. Occasionally he traveled to Salzburg to see Anna Bernhard, who attended a school for midwifery at the local hospital. To have a proper profession was, in her eyes, the only way to support a family, so that Freumbichler could live a life dedicated to literature. For Freumbichler this solution was very convenient. In February 1913 he had turned to Mrs. Thomsen, who was willing to help and pay for his wife's apprenticeship (290 Kronen), under one condition: Freumbichler had to find work to support Anna Bernhard. Mrs. Thomsen did not agree with the idea that Anna Bernhard sacrifice everything for the writer. On February 24, 1913 she wrote to Johannes Freumbichler: "It is impossible to leave all the burden on this fragile woman. She would soon break under it and then your family would be in deepest misery. All the artists and writers I know pursue a profession more or less intensely . . . Unfortunately you failed to do this and now, of course, it is rather difficult . . . In my opinion your talent will unfold only with the burden of your daily sorrows out of the way . . . All support from another person will always cause problems, is haphazard and will never give you the strength and satisfaction that

Anna Bernhard (ca. 1913)

a man gains from being self-sufficient" (1913/14).

In mid-July 1913 Anna Bernhard was ready to pass her exam. Immediately after, Freumbichler wanted to return to Bozen with her. He had hoped that Mrs. Thomsen would introduce him to the proper circles. However, she could not fulfill his expectations, because she led a very secluded life and did not have the kind of contacts Freumbichler could have used. "Above all, it would be better, especially for your wife, to move to a larger city where the opportunities are more favorable," she wrote to Johannes Freumbichler on July 23, 1913. Mrs. Thomsen advised him expressly to choose Vienna.

VIENNA

September 1913 to July 1916

Since September 5, 1913 Johannes Freumbichler had been registered in Vienna, living at Vienna XIII, Barchettigassse 11/8. As of December 1914 he stayed at Vienna III, Schanzgasse 21/2, and in mid-February 1915 he moved back to the 13th district, to Flötzersteig 49/4 where he worked as a clerk with the municipality of Vienna from February 1914 to July 10, 1916. With the termination of his employment he also gave up his residence at Flötzersteig.

In August of 1914 Freumbichler completed the tale "Peter and Mary" ("Peter und Maria"). Kasparek wrote: "For the time being it (PaM) would probably not receive high honors, but it allows us to hope for a better future" (1914/14). Mrs. Thomsen's hope was small, for she thought she knew the reason for Freumbichler's failure:

53

At three in the morning, together with the bakers and railway workers, he got up and sat down to write. (Ke 100)

The lifelong habit of getting up early and almost always before five o'clock I inherited from my grandfather. The ritual is repeated, the seasons are countered through the same daily discipline, against the incessant powers of lethargy and with the constant awareness that all action is only senseless action. (Ke 149)

". . . if he only worked on shorter and more delicate pieces. These times do not accommodate endless novels, everything today is constantly changing and moving fast" (1915/12). Often enough she would urge Freumbichler to act with more determination, so as not to burden his family too much with his luckless endeavors. She also conceived her personal support as being ill-used: "The help can never be effective, and the helper does not get joy from helping because he sees that his help is useless" (1915/12).

In her opinion Freumbichler should have tried to build a firm basis, for "nobody knows in advance whether he was born to be a great artist or poet, and besides one can be mistaken about one's abilities" (ibid.).

Despite this critical remark Mrs. Thomsen sent money to the Freumbichler family in March 1915 in order to make a contribution to the fulfillment of the "Ziegentraum" ("goat dream"). Freumbichler wanted to live in an outlying district of Vienna, raising goats and bees and growing potatoes to alleviate the food shortages. In August 1915, when Freumbichler had to ask Mrs. Thomsen again for money, he promised her to put even greater demands on himself, to "inflict the hardest tasks" on himself: "I rise daily at four o'clock in the morning to work" (1915/10). As a grateful gesture he wanted to dedicate the novel "Happiness at Aringhof" (*Das Glück am Aringhof*) to her. Mrs. Thomsen, however, was willing to support him this time only if he accepted a prospective civil servant's position. Obviously the clerical position with the municipality of Vienna did not seem secure enough to her. In order to give her the impression that her support was not in vain, he informed her about his literary plans: "Apart from the subject drafts I am also revising the published novel thoroughly.

Artistically it has no value at all. However, it can be excused due to my youth and the difficult path I had to follow. Now I begin to comprehend what it means to create a work of art, and I hope to write several books of lasting value in the years to come" (1915/10).

Richard Pokorny, Vienna XII, Rotenmühlgasse 28, typed Freumbichler's manuscripts into fair copy (1916/10).

Aside from the money received from Bozen, the Freumbichler family was also supported by relatives from Henndorf who sent butter, flour, bacon, potatoes and eggs (1916/1). His sister, Marie Russ, helped in Vienna, where Johannes Freumbichler would come to eat on weekends at her house at Ballgasse. During the years in Vienna Anna Bernhard worked as a maid or nurse in a number of households. Since she often had to stay with the patients, Freumbichler was forced to do housework himself during the week. He found the household chores next to his literary work rather disturbing, and with this attitude he nurtured strong feelings of guilt in Anna Bernhard. She wanted to help support the family with her work, but she was also needed by her husband at home. She feared causing even more troubles for him: "Even if I have to suffer and to go without so much, it will never make up for what I have caused you to suffer through me" (AB-JF/13). Moreover, his wife's self-reproaches obstructed his intellectual work. He responded: "You constantly destroy my courageous mood, which is essential for my work. Once I lose courage, it takes me weeks, even months to regain my balance . . . So listen: Holiest duty and order given by the head of the family: Never again a single word on such matters!" (JF/1).

Rudolf Kasparek (1916)

Anna Bernhard was not only concerned about Johannes Freumbichler, but also about the artist and mutual friend Rudolf Kasparek: "It grieves me to see Rudolf so unhappy, even more so since I cannot help him. Oh, could I only, with my hands' work, bring freedom to all poor artists" (AB-JF/13).

Rudolf Kasparek 1914-1919

In March 1914 Kasparek moved to Innsbruck where he lived in the "Gasthaus zur Alten Post," at the so-called "Kineschlößl," a "small castle" located at Schulgasse 3. He worked temporarily for the Royal Railways in a laboratory. When he was given notice, he started work in early 1915 as an unskilled laborer in a nitric acid factory (1914/17). At the same time, he also moved to the "Försterhaus Schupfen" in the Brennerstraße.

Kasparek, who felt very lonely, suffered from depression frequently. To make it worse, the events of the war dampened his spirits even more. He was not so much moved by political questions as by the fate of the individual soldier. Many had lost their lives in the war. "And it touches me most that all of them, truly every single one! was not aware of his life. One can hardly stand to think about it" (1914/14).

The new position in Innsbruck was not to Kasparek's liking either. However, he admitted that he was to be greatly blamed for his present situation, because "I detested each and every job and I should have gladly accepted every chance, and, quite the contrary, I was only happy to learn that luckily nothing had come out of it again; that I preferred to beg, feigned being sick, became a liar rather than carry the burden of this abomination . . ." (1914/17).

He wanted to change his situation by going to Vienna to see Johannes Freumbichler to "reconnect" both their lives. His circumstances, however, were so difficult that soon he had to renounce this wish (1914/15 and 16). His health had reached an alarming state. Constantly breathing nitric acid at his workplace was poison for his lungs. Eventually his sister Bertha had to nurse him (1915/9).

His sole comfort was his relationship with a girl called Erika "who knows all my futility and poverty and who shrugs it all off and only wants me. In the past few days this has been a heavy load to bear, for I am ill and worse off than she thinks" (1914/17).

In December 1914, Kasparek already felt terminally ill and was convinced that he would "probably die soon" (1914/17). Kasparek suffered from tuberculosis. The lack of money did not allow him to take advantage of an opportunity to go south. He lost a potential position in Bozen due to his medical evaluation. Toward the end of 1914 he wrote to Freumbichler: "Again I find myself quite discouraged in this cold northern town, and I have to fend off winter without the slighest appropriate means. This will certainly end in disaster" (1914/17).

In the same letter to Freumbichler of December 28, 1914, Kasparek therefore enclosed his last will "bearing in mind the miserable outcome of my life." I would like to present these provisions in their unabridged form because they might, apart from Kasparek's literary work, also reveal traces in the search for his unpublished works.

     1. As I also told Wilhelm v. Kleinschmitt, my edition "Fr. Young Ballads" ("Fr. junge Lieder") by Huber, including the dedications, is to be destroyed. I hope K. will eventually be in a position

to use the remaining 150 marks to buy them. If not, it will be you, for there is plenty of time, since nothing of it is being sold anyhow.

One thing that remains to be tried is to pulp the collection, so we would not have to pay for it. Regarding a second edition, which will combine the revised part with some new ideas and which will be prepared by myself as far as possible, I would like to say that this should not be done before either you or Kleinschmitt have found a well-known publisher at no cost. I want to have—this will have to be taken care of by you—the manuscript in two copies, one of which to be kept by yourself, the other by the publisher, and I will start working on it right away. Should I be interrupted, be advised that nothing else shall be included except for what is marked with the red sign "*" which I will use with possible comments wherever it deserves to be. Where you do not see it, please follow the comments. As far as the sequence (order of the poems) is concerned, this is also up to you both. In general, I ask you not to miss any kind of cooperation, even if it is just for an exchange of ideas.

2. My attempts at prose, which are few and almost entirely in need of revision, I will leave to your discretion, i.e., if you wish, burn them, as I have done to a number of them. I feel attached to one draft only: "Uncle Herbert and His Bride" ("Onkel Herbert und seine Braut"). Please read it with affection, scrutinize it, and, if possible, finish it according to the suggestions. Otherwise, I would not object to having it printed as a fragment.

3. My notes, remarks, aphorisms, ideas, etc. should be separated from all this garbage and maybe

combined with prose or letters to make a small book.

4. My correspondence with you is ready to be used by yourself as you wish. However, it is not in order. Partly it will have to be destroyed, in part it might be useful for a portrayal of my life and above all, it will help you biographically. So do with it what you want!

Apart from this there is little more to say. I have fared poorly with my life; therefore this miserable fiasco, . . . this is an attitude which a normal mind cannot judge—but it was of course the reason for my failure" (1914/17).

Kasparek also asked Freumbichler, for their friendship's sake, to "do something for the better part of posterity by looking back at me in a biography and thus assuring me a monument through you" (ibid.).

Five months later, his girlfriend Erika left him (1919/9). He hoped to be dismissed in Innsbruck in order to enlist in the army despite his serious illness. Vienna would offer an opportunity to finally see his friend, "in spite of these unfavorable times" (1916/13). This letter of June 25, 1916 is of particular interest to me as the editor of Johannes Freumbichler's correspondence, because it shows that Freumbichler himself thought of editing the letters.

After 1 1/2 years I have finally rescued my belongings and your letters. I will sort them step by step, a thing which has not been done yet. Do you believe that the stench of the underworld, which creeps towards me so disgustingly from all those boxes, can be blown away, or will it be you alone

who will enjoy the sun? You have signed with your full name, i.e., you have come to realize that it has some value. I have to follow your example, with you, in the correspondence, even if you edit without me. After all, be concerned also with the spiritual welfare of your friend Rudolf Kasparek (1916/13).

Kasparek was, in fact, considered fit for military service. He himself saw the irony of it. In October 1916, having just arrived in Vienna, he was sent to Kagran to the Section of Reconvalescents, No. 47 of the Royal Infantry Regiment No. 84 (1916/16). In mid-November 1916 he was sent back to Tyrol. His new residence was in Mieders. His lung disease was accompanied by severe bouts of migraine and he felt to be destined also "for spiritual death" (1916/18). As he had been very active with his literary work in Innsbruck, this prospect he found unbearable.

In the summer of 1916, he had worked on a narrative with a protagonist by the name of "Wegmacher Karl." Already envisioning the published book, he had written to Freumbichler: "Even the rich, who certainly will not like reading it, can be allowed to see that man basically does not need much more and that the rest is luxury which should be distributed more generously" (1916/15).

Three Munich narratives were ready to print and he forwarded them to Freumbichler for editing purposes. One of these narratives had been written on the occasion of Paul Heyse's death (April 2, 1914 in Munich). Kasparek also wanted to continue with "Uncle Robert, . . . who was left behind in Bernried, who did not prosper in Munich for lack of nutrition, and who, for the same reason was hiding in a cocoon in Innsbruck,

where he is still waiting. Maybe I can develop him this time and finally put him to sleep. The stories that I promised you recently were interrupted because of him; his completion would be all the more welcome" (1916/15).

In July 1917, the series of ballads, "Lady Lilo," was nearing completion (1917/10). In the same month Kasparek sent Freumbichler the narrative "The Tailor in Despair" ("Der Schneider in Verzweiflung") to be edited. It is remarkable that as early as February 1914 Kasparek intended to write a comedy which was to be titled either "The Tailor in Despair" or "The Lucky Pot" ("Der Topf des Glücks"). At that time he had suggested to Freumbichler that he collaborate on this project. Freumbichler apparently had not reacted to this idea, which for Kasparek had meant "a perfect salvation" (1914/18). A copy of the "Tailor" for the *M.N.N.* (*Münchner Neueste Nachrichten*) was returned (1917/5). The poem "Erika" was to be edited by Freumbichler who sent it back in April 1917 with harsh criticism. Dr. Horsch, one of Kasparek's patrons from the Munich period, could not do anything either for "Erika" (1919/5).

In Mieders, Kasparek edited Mrs. Thomsen's fairy tales (1917/17).

At Easter 1917, Kasparek received a confirmation of exemption from military service due to his lung disease (1917/4).

The burdens were mounting. His sister Bertha, who was unemployed in Vienna, used up one third of Kasparek's "revenues" (1917/10). In September 1917, Kasparek had to leave his quarters in Mieders. His wish of going to Meran was again not feasible (1917/14). Therefore he moved to the "Poet's House," a pavilion on the eastern outskirts of Mieders without light and water. He

also lacked the money to buy food, and his hunger was often so overwhelming that he could hardly do intellectual work (1917/17). He played with the idea of earning money by making artistic enlargements of photographs of war casualties and selling these in Rosina Schlager's store in Henndorf (1917/16), but this plan did not work out either.

In the fall of 1919, Rudolf Kasparek vomited blood and he was brought to a heated hotel room in Mieders where he remarked: "One can hardly think to an end the egoistic mediocrity of people. Couldn't these people have thought of giving me this room a long time ago?" (1919/6).

Transport to a hospital was too dangerous, and Kasparek did not want to be brought to the Innsbruck hospital, for "the atmosphere of such a house is to me anything but happy, and the lack of tact in setting up tabernacles all over the place and saying loud prayers everywhere (even in the early morning when one has just fallen asleep) has tortured me enough already in February 1917" (1919/6). He was nursed in the hotel.

On November 30, 1919, Kasparek wrote his last letter to Johannes Freumbichler: "Winter with its harshness will soon have taken me . . . The nights are truly an ordeal. The morning, mostly complete exhaustion and only toward half past ten, after having been up for a while and lying for half an hour on the sofa, do I begin to feel more like a human being, but once in a while maybe I will seek refuge in a letter . . . In short, it is too cold here even to die. Let me greet you meanwhile, I hope you write again eventually—and I hope you do not suffer from the cold as much as your nocturnal puppet RK." (1919/6)

Rudolf Kasparek to Johannes Freumbichler (30 November 1919)

Kasparek pursued literary thoughts only when fantasizing in his fever: "The poet in me has almost vanished. Only in feverish nights, as long as terrible manlike distorted grimaces do not haunt me, is he active now and then. But everything is getting lost; there is only one thing I want to think of: the plan for a rather popular, or better, common comedy, to which somebody expressly motivated and summoned me in my fever" (ibid.).

When Rudolf Kasparek wrote this last letter to Freumbichler, he was thirty-three years old. He died on January 27, 1920 in Mieders.

VIENNA

July 1916 - December 1934

At the end of July 1916 Johannes Freumbichler and Anna Bernhard moved to Wernhardstraße 6/3/13 in Vienna XVI.

The children, Hertha and Farald, spent the greater part of the war years with relatives in Henndorf. They helped "Aunt Rosa," who due to leg problems was frequently confined to bed, with the business and the boarding house. This arrangement relieved the strain on the parents in this economic crisis, which primarily affected the big cities.

Still, Johannes Freumbichler was dependent on Mrs. Thomsen's support. She continued to send money despite her disappointment with Johannes Freumbichler, who did "not show any literary success" (1916/24). Although she was enthusiastic about the manuscript of *Eduard Aring* ("The depiction of rural life at the Aringhof is very

lovely and the short village stories well observed,"
(1916/22), she had again financed an unpublished project. In December 1917 Freumbichler sent her the narrative "The Spy" ("Der Spion").

The literary works of the last two war years were not
published until the beginning of 1918. The narratives
"The Night in the Brothel" ("Die Nacht im Lusthause"),
"The Wedding Night" ("Die Hochzeitsnacht"), and "The
Vision" ("Traumbild") appeared in the Berlin weekly
German Novel Magazine and Library, 54th year. A
printing of *Eduard Aring* began with issue no.17.

From October to December 1918, Johannes Freumbichler worked as a clerk with the Austrian industrial
company Warchalowski Eissler & Co.

In the summer of 1919 he met Franz Karl Ginzkey
(1919/5). In November 1919 the narrative "The Devil's
Mill" ("Satansmühle") was published in the *Novel
Magazine* (1919/7).

In 1919 Hertha and Farald went off on their own.
Farald was employed with Justin Bischof in Grub in the
canton of St. Gallen (Switzerland), while Hertha worked
as a maid in Zurich until August 1921.

On November 14, 1920, Maria Freumbichler died at
the age of seventy. All her life she had supported her
son. Freumbichler had often sent her printed or
unpublished material. One year prior to her death she
had congratulated her son on his birthday with the
following: "Dear Hans! It has been thirty-eight years
since you were born. You have lived through a lot, few
good and many bad things. May God grant that it will
get better now. Pray to Him, have faith in Him, and He
will help you, and you will have more luck than so far.
Fate is often strange. I wish you a very happy birthday,
be merry, and don't disappoint your family. One always

has to think of better times, otherwise one can't be happy. May God grant that your work succeeds. Many greetings, mother" (1919/4). On his mother's letter of December 22, 1913, Johannes Freumbichler had marked in the margin: "Oh God! Our correspondence! The joyful bliss it breathes!" (1913/4).

His father, Joseph Freumbichler, had died on June 1, 1909.

After the war it was difficult for Mrs. Thomsen to send parcels and money to Vienna. Since southern Tyrol was no longer part of Austria, there were frequent and time-consuming complications with customs.

In 1920 Mrs. Thomsen put up a painter in the "Wendtland-Villa" in Gries: he was a student of Egger-Lienz (1920/7). Another protegé, a painter by the name of Hepperger, later received the State Medal in Graz in 1923 (1923/2).

Anna Bernhard's regular income was still the only way that Johannes Freumbichler could devote himself exclusively to writing. However, her sacrifice and her understanding for his artistic work were not made easy for her; he was constantly angered because he had to take care of the household by himself (1920/8). Freumbichler wanted to be able to "breathe" and therefore he thought of bringing Hertha back from Switzerland. She was supposed to do the housework for him, while he could teach her punctuation and shorthand so that at a later date she would be able to work as a clerk (1920/8). If his daughter looked after him, he would not object to Anna Bernhard working out of the house and in this way supporting the family. Her work would be the prerequisite for his carefree tranquility that was so essential to his success. He wrote: "I also plan for us to have a secure future so that we do not end up in slavery.

77

However, this will only be possible if you stay for some time and if you save all of your income down to the last penny" (1920/8). He limited the time he needed to build a future to one year: "Oh, if I only have this one year to breathe freely, our fate will take a complete turn" (ibid.).

Although Anna Bernhard did not live at Wernhardstraße in the summer months of 1921, but instead ran Mrs. Konetschny's household at Karolinengasse 14/1, Johannes Freumbichler went to Kaiserleiten (near Henndorf) in mid-July in order to "write in peace" (1921/13). He stayed at a farm, going for frequent walks (1921/8) and eating lunch at the "Gerbl" inn (1921/7).

His literary efforts in Kaiserleiten were productive. On July 21 he finished the theatrical play *Das Opfer* (The Victim) and, a few days later, a novella (1921/11). Mrs. Bauer typed the fair copy of the drama (1921/17) and Johannes Freumbichler sent the script to Max Mell in Pernegg. On August 28, 1921 Max Mell responded. He was convinced of Freumbichler's talent; however, he believed "that it will not be the piece to bring success, since the topic is not anything one would dare to produce." The play was too revolutionary and too biased. A possible venue to perform the play might have been the "Volksbühne" in Andritz, but "to propagate a hero who prefers shooting himself to becoming a clergyman would definitely have seemed too aggressive toward the church. And this was one thing no theater director would have dared do. Apart from this the audience would have rather seen an active than a lonely character. "The supporting characters are very intriguing, all of them are lively, pleasant! You definitely have what it takes to be a dramatist, keep on writing with joy, you will manage to have another successful play, a farmer's character is

The child whom the father, in his lifelong quest for art, had sent not to an ordinary but to the highly renowned Vienna Ballet School in order to have her trained as a dancer at the "Hofoper" and pursue the career of a ballerina, and who had been able to escape from this ballet ordeal forced upon her by the ambitious father only through a sudden and violent illness. (A 120)

far better expressed by you than by anybody else" (1921/6).

In August 1920 Freumbichler had already informed Mrs. Thomsen of his plan concerning this play (1920/5). Almost eighteen months later, without having read *Das Opfer*, as had Max Mell, she commented on the finished play: "If I am not mistaken, you were working on a theater play. It is probably very difficult to hit the right tone at once, especially since you are not one to work on best sellers for the audience, particularly today's audiences. There is certainly something special necessary to work for the theater, but you will most likely continue in this field" (1921/2).

Johannes Freumbichler received Mrs. Thomsen's last letter on December 18, 1923 (1923/3).

On August 2, 1921 Freumbichler started the novella "The Mandarin Carver" ("Der Mandarinenschnitzer") (1921/11).

Only now did Hertha stop working in Zurich; on her way home she visited her father in Kaiserleiten. There seemed to be a mutual understanding that Freumbichler would take over her savings accumulated in Switzerland (1921/15). Freumbichler had never fully accepted the fact that Hertha was working as a maid. He preferred envisioning her as a ballet dancer in Vienna (1921/6, 1922/3).

On August 15, 1921 Johannes Freumbichler and Hertha traveled to Vienna.

Although Anna Bernhard did everything in her power to avert the most pressing financial problems, she felt Freumbichler's discontent: "I feel as if I do find a warm stove at home, but not a warm heart" (1922/1). But she also bore this pain for his sake: "The thought of how to liberate you completely is on my mind day and night.

81

Johannes Freumbichler to Anna
Bernhard (12 August 1922)

82

How much you must have suffered inwardly to become what you are today. Your way must be mine or else life will have lost its meaning for me" (ibid.).

Starting in July 1922, Anna Bernhard worked as a nurse with Mrs. Strnad who owned an inn in Rabensburg in Lower Austria. And Freumbichler wrote: "I am sitting in my cell, writing my novel and thinking of you always" (1922/2).

When his sister Rosina in Henndorf was confined to her bed in summer and therfore unable to attend to her guests, she asked her brother to send Hertha to help her. Freumbichler did not allow this, for he could "not exist alone" (1922/3).

The economic crisis of these years had a profound effect on Freumbichler too. "How ridiculous and humiliating this misery is," he wrote to Anna Bernhard in July 1922 (1922/6). Prices increased by the day: "What will come out of all this?" (1922/9). Now Anna Bernhard had to persevere so that his literary plans could be realized.

Freumbichler was working on a novel: "The novel proceeds nicely, and I do not think I am wrong to say that this time it will be something outstanding. But there is still a lot to overcome" (1922/9). Apart from this he intended to print the "Salzburg Ballads" ("Salzburger Lieder") in the spring of 1921 "on his own!" (1922/16). The profusion of notebooks was another reason not to give up. "My notebooks are filled with so many treasures, that to despair would simply be outright foolishness." And again, he asked for more time: "Give me two years of living carefree and I will give you a kingdom" (ibid.).

Since there seemed to be no change in sight, Freumbichler perceived his lack of success to be a consequence of the disorganized household. Now he would

All his life he made the ones around him suffer, in particular his wife, my grandmother, and also my mother, who both had enabled him through their energetic support to live in a state of complete creative isolation. They had paid from their own lives, and they could not have paid a higher price. (Ke 100)

But they all respected him like no other person and they made it possible for him to do what he wanted and they loved him. They believed in him and they guarded his privacy. (Ke 102)

have preferred Anna Bernhard to stay home. In the fall of 1922 he thought of buying two knitting machines so that she would be able to make money from her home as of fall 1922. However, she was supposed to run the household "quietly" (1922/14). On September 14, 1922 Anna Bernhard left employment in Rabensburg (1922/19).

In late summer of 1924, Anna Bernhard was forced to work as a nurse again. From September on she worked in Pritzleinsdorf near Vienna (1924/1), but she stayed only for one month. From October 1924 until the beginning of 1925 she was employed by Mrs. Agathe Kornfeld, Vienna 18, Julienstraße 38. In January 1925 Freumbichler completed a novel (1925/2).

In December 1926, Anna Bernhard stayed with Erich and Lotte Bruckmann in Probstdorf in Grossenzersdorf where she worked as a nurse for the young woman and also looked after her two children (1927/16). During this time Johannes Freumbichler lived alone at Wernhardstraße, for Hertha also had outside employment. Anna Bernhard was able to see him only on her days off to do the laundry and clean the flat. On weekends Freumbichler still ate at his sister Marie's. Her son Roland, who worked for the *Arbeiterzeitung*, was a painter like his father (1927/19), and Fernanda was a dancer.

When Anna Bernhard started her new work in Probstdorf in December 1926, Freumbichler again marked a "new beginning": "And as far as I am concerned, I am starting right now, at this holy moment, to wrap myself into a cocoon, but so thoroughly and seriously as maybe never before in my life; what I strive for has to happen, or else life will have no meaning at all. To attain this goal, I will need your complete and unreserved support and devotion" (1926/4).

Anna Bernhard (1943)

Since 1925 Hertha had worked at Mrs. Handofsky's in Vienna (1927/44). She also supported her father with monthly payments.

Despite all the support Freumbichler was overwhelmed by weariness and the loathsomeness of life. The disgraceful chore of having to see the pawnbroker for a typewriter, shoes, suit or coat often depressed him: "There is still this powerful poison in me, which, despite all efforts, I have not been able to get out. It is the poison of failure. Often I pass hours filled with deepest horror," he wrote on January 20, 1927 (1927/20). But he would not give up. Four days later he started a new novel. One hundred thirty of the "Salzburg Ballads" were completed.

The correspondence between Johannes Freumbichler and Anna Bernhard during the years 1927 and 1928 is a unique document of Freumbichler's ever-changing moods. "The underlying evil is the lack of security and comfort, the prerequisites for me to excel in my field," he wrote in February 1927 (1927/23). Anna Bernhard's attitude remained the same. She encouraged her husband in days of spiritual despair, strongly believing in his artistic talent. She wrote to him: "You have sunk into a state of low spirits and often I feel this fear, oh, this oppressive fear. Do not despair, the day must come for you to free yourself from the dark nights of your prison. I think that you are brooding too much. If you throw away your precious life, people will say with sympathy, well he was a weakling. I will give everything to you, if only you exist and live. One day it will be known who you are. Go on writing, do not bear a grudge against the humans who contaminate this world. Write for the unborn life . . . I am only a weak woman, but

The material misery was harsh in a time of the highest unemployment rates and the suicide rate at its peak. My grandfather supposedly threatened to commit suicide every day and to have kept a loaded pistol under his pillow. (Ki 63/64)

I feel strong enough to serve as a support for you to lean on . . . Think of me who sees in you nothing but that which is pure, noble and great" (1927/21).

Freumbichler gained strength once more from the thought of an all new beginning: ". . . I felt so miserable all week! But at the risk of your laughing at me, let me tell you that I will resume my task, the purpose of my life, as if I were starting all over again. All I need is the courage I had in Meran and later, and I will reach my goal. We will not be able to expect any financial advantages before one or two years" (1927/27). Anna Bernhard expected nothing. Her view of their lives went beyond material values: "The exulting feelings I have by being at your side cannot be suppressed by poverty, misery, and outer disappointment. Let us march on, hand in hand, be it towards good luck or disaster. You will reach your goal yet . . . But be that as it may, an overpowering fate like ours must have its beautiful side as well" (1927/31).

In April 1927, Johannes Freumbichler, discouraged, again tried a new beginning. The "empty coal basket" (1927/36) disgruntled him. The coming of spring was to invigorate his creative spirits. "I will hold out for one or two weeks, and then I will make the greatest efforts to start over again. I must not lose another day. Hertha knows what I expect from her on the first of the month, without exception" (ibid.). And again he allowed himself the deadline of another year: "I am resolved to throw away my life if I cannot force a change within one year. It is a dirty (literally) existence, I am sick of it . . . It is written in the stars whether our efforts deserve fulfillment or not. And if not, I will want to see the dice rolling. My heart seems to be dead already, torn to pieces by too much brooding, it does not seem to feel anything

Johannes Freumbichler to Anna
Bernhard (8 May 1927)

anymore" (1927/36). Anna Bernhard answered to his despondency immediately: "I ask you, I can only implore you, get on with it. Oh, if I could only manage to lead you through this maze of melancholy and despair. Listen to the voice of your divine power. You fight God and you fight the devil. Don't let yourself be brought down. You are here to accomplish a great task and now you are weary of the way. I believe in you and my admiration for you fills me like religion the believer. I want to stand by you in these difficult days" (1927/37).

A few days later, Dr. Drasenaric of Graz asked Johannes Freumbichler to supply a story for a calendar. The publisher Speidel rejected a novella collection; however, he asked for a novel because: "Now would be a favorable time for a publication" (1927/38). Immediately he forwarded the revised novel typoscript of *Jörg Hoffegott* to Mrs. Vagacs to type the fair copy (Vienna VII, Kandlgasse 35/11). He wrote to Anna Bernhard: "The publication of the novel would be so encouraging that all our hopes may still come true. After all that has happened my belief is weak, very, very weak . . . However, I don't have a choice but to write with new drafts despite deepest poverty, discouragement, the abominable situation my family lives in, which tears apart my heart every day, yes, every hour, despite my weakened body, lasting helplessness and meekness" (1927/38). He emphatically repeated the demands that he had made on himself two weeks earlier: "For another year I will give everything" (ibid.).

And again, three weeks later: ". . . this disgusting environment, these ugly rooms and all this lousy misery are like constant and easily visible weights pulling me down. But as always: one year of best efforts! Then I will see further!" (1927/40). One day later he wanted to

. . . he had isolated himself and with himself, in the course of time, his entire environment, his wife, my mother and her husband and their children, and in this way also myself; my grandfather had been completely incapable of making contact and had been isolated from all of them, no matter which background, which social standing, which character they had. (Ke 104/105)

Isolation is for long periods of time a complete isolation of body and mind; by subduing myself entirely and unerringly to my needs I can cope with myself. (Ke 149/150)

He was supposed to become a priest and a bishop and originally he wanted to be a politician, socialist, communist and like everybody trying to write, he became disappointed with all these impossible classifications, and became a writer philosophizing about these categories and idiocies and philosophies and naturally a loner absorbed in his writing. (Ke 99/100)

He was not an expressive man and he hated society. He had imprisoned himself with his work, his life's work of writing, yet he had allowed himself the freedom of being alone and subordinating everything else. (Ke 100)

start all over again: "Now I want to reorganize my whole intellectual being and when this is done, in a few weeks, I want to make a fresh start" (1927/41). Drasenaric took one calendar story and one poem (1927/41).

For a short time, Freumbichler's self-confidence reached unknown heights. On reading one of his poems from the "Salzburg Ballads," he remarked: "This will live longer than a thousand years" (ibid.).

In July 1927 the fair copy of the novel was finished. He sent *Jörg Hoffegott* to the Deutscher Verlag (1927/47). Max Mell encouraged him (1927/59), but Freumbichler had little hope: "I am completely isolated and this is my misfortune" (1927/47). However, he started a new project despite everything: "I took up working on a new novel, but if fate doesn't have mercy, where will it end?" (ibid.).

To Anna Bernhard he wrote words which also held true for himself: "Do not long for freedom. Accept the state you are in as a necessity and you will not suffer. If I give in to this misery that you can probably only imagine, I will not live tomorrow" (1927/48). This hopelessness nurtured thorough contempt for human beings in him: "We must pretend outside as if we had sympathy, but inside we must be completely untouched. If you want to survive in this world, you have to don a shell of crudeness. Most people, by far most of them, do not need such a shell, for they are crude right through by nature. One has to limit one's feelings only to a few, and if nobody is worth it, to nobody. I am falling into indefinite hatred for people" (1927/64).

Turned away from society, he put even more efforts into writing. In the new year he wanted to print the "Alpenländischen": "Thus we have made the first step to

He was a loner, he was incapable of dealing with people, thus unsuitable for any kind of employment. Up to the age of fifty-five he had earned practically nothing. He lived off his wife and daughter who believed in him blindly. (Ki 66/67)

realize our project, and we will accomplish it as long as we keep up strength and stamina," he wrote on September 6, 1927.

Two weeks later Freumbichler had to stop again (1927/67). Spiritually he was in no position to work. Anna Bernhard cheered him up: "It may well be the tragedy of your genius that you have to be so alone, so lonely and unhappy. As far as your momentary lack of spirit goes, an improvement in living conditions will take care of it" (1927/68).

Anna Bernhard's circumstances were better. The Bruckmann family spoiled her, and she did not suffer from poverty. She was treated like a member of the family; one allowed her to be present when guests from the "Sachsengang" castle were invited, and she participated eagerly in conversations on art. From her personal experience she was familiar with the peculiarities of an artist. And she knew her task: "An artist's wife has to be a genius, too, and be the synthesis of a dozen women. One has to be able to hide one's desire for affection when he covers himself with a veil of coldness. It hurts, one feels helpless, meaningless. An artist only loves his art and this makes an egoist of him. A noble egoist. He forgets what is around him and one only follows after, but he won't allow you right next to him. He falls prey to his moods and is always under tension, cannot live with ties, not with even the most tender one. One has to let him do what he wants to do without asking why. Expect nothing, give everything, sit still when he is torn by his moods, and be with him in his bright moments. The highest duty is to love him despite all this from the bottom of one's heart and leave one's own needs aside. He will not change" (1927/68). An article on similar marriages almost one year later caused her to

say proudly: "I read it with keen interest. Such famous men and such mean women" (1928/24). In the same letter of June 22, 1928 Anna Bernhard appeared as a liberal woman: "The majority of women could never show their true self to their husbands, for to show sensuality was strictly forbidden. Women have never felt differently from today's women, they were just never allowed to express it: this is how we are. Today, one may be, next to wife and mother, also the man's lover" (ibid.). This was surprising, because Johannes Freumbichler had decided seven months earlier due to his lack of success: "We must . . . live more like friends . . . and focus on one thing: my work! Let us stand together, firmly and thoroughly, then we will—I am sure of it—reach a victorious goal" (1927/75). Anna Bernhard agreed: "I came to you and I will stay with you, no matter what happens. I demand nothing, I renounce everything, but you must not hold me in contempt as a useless creature . . . Oh, if I could only help, rescue you before it is too late" (1927/76).

Johannes Freumbichler worked even more intensely, getting up daily at three o'clock in the morning to write. In the afternoons he would go for long walks to Breitensee and retire to sleep early.

In November 1927 the "Salzburg Ballads" were complete. Mrs. Vagacs typed them into fair copy. *Jörg Hoffegott* was returned by the Deutscher Verlag, but Anna Bernhard played down the disappointment: "There will be a time, or rather, a man who will realize who stands before him" (1927/72). Because the novel had been rejected, Johannes Freumbichler wanted Anna Bernhard to stay home again, in order to work more efficiently with "regular meals" (1927/76). He advertised in a paper for a child that his wife could nurse at home.

Although Anna Bernhard did not want to leave Probstdorf she gave in to her husband's wishes: "I don't care what I do, but what you do. My dear, we have to invest all our strength. Hertha and I have to do everything possible or else give up our lives" (1928/16).

On May 28, 1928 Dr. Ernst Haeckel from Budapest contacted Johannes Freumbichler. He had read the "Salzburg Ballads" and wanted to use them for a scholarly project on Austrian regional poetry (1928/4). In July 1928 he included some of the ballads in his publication (1928/25).

Anna Bernhard did not quit her employment in Probstdorf right away. Therefore she found Johannes Freumbichler depressed on visiting him in Vienna: "Everytime I came to see you I thought continually of what to do, how I could help you, but I couldn't find a way out. I know only one thing. You have to live. Show the world more of the riches that up to now only I could enjoy. A man of such intellect must not go down in misery" she writes on May 23, 1928 (1928/21).

In October 1928 she left the Bruckmann family and accepted employment with "Mrs. Hedda" in Vienna-Mödling, Bergstraße 6, but as of September 1929 she began staying at home. She wanted to make ends meet by sewing. She knew that Freumbichler's success depended much on her efforts alone. "Our 'child' has commanded much too much time, we will embrace it and protect it. With my determination I will succeed in bringing our ship that has been repaired a thousand times, to shore. You, my love, have courage and try to work. We must love each other deeply and put our minds to the most beautiful task" (1929/18).

The daughter was expected to make her career in the most renowned theaters in the country and, indeed, as I know, she fulfilled all the necessary requirements, but she ended up wiping off dust in the front rooms and the private rooms of the nouveaux riches in Döbling and also in various kitchens in and around the Währinger Hauptstraße. (Ki 62)

She had indeed, as she herself had said, been enslaved to her father, and her love had never been responded to with the same intensity, which made her suffer all her life. My grandfather had not been a good father to his children, he had in fact never had any serious relationship with his family and was never able to, just as he had never had a home, for his home had always been his mind, and his family had been the great thinkers. With these thoughts he felt at home and comforted as nowhere else, as he once said. (A 120/121)

. . . my father, the farmer's son and carpenter, had deserted her and had no longer taken care of her and me. Toward the end of the war he was murdered, beaten to death in Frankfurt/Oder, under which circumstances I could never find out. I had heard this from his father, my paternal grandfather, whom I saw only once in my life as opposed to my father whom I never saw in my life. (U 127/128)

The invisible man, who was said at times to consist merely of lies and meanness, was the lifelong spoilsport. (Ki 40)

Hertha Bernhard 1927-1934

From 1927 to 1929 Hertha Bernhard worked in Vienna as a maid with various families. She regarded it her human duty to do everything to allow her father a carefree existence for his literary work. Like Anna Bernhard, the daughter helped with strong inner affection. Once she wrote to Johannes Freumbichler: "Sunday, and I am alone. I feel like writing you something very nice, but when you are sad, so am I. Just now I felt we were one being who either lives or has to die. I already regretted having spent time on Thursday with such loud and dumb company, but with you, even when you don't smile, it is much more beautiful and every time I feel richer inside" (HB-JF/22).

In the summer of 1930 Hertha Bernhard was pregnant. Anna Bernhard wrote to Johannes Freumbichler on September 15, 1930: "Be that as it may, she is our child and we must not leave her . . . I will not forget that for many years she has always done her best for us, always enjoyed being able to give you a good meal and often helped us in great misery . . . For this reason we have to help her wherever we can" (1930/1). Since the child would be born out of wedlock, Hertha Bernhard had to leave Vienna. She received an address in the Netherlands where she was supported by Mrs. Weiss from Rotterdam, Shied van Musshenbrokstraat 18a. During her pregnancy Hertha Bernhard worked for a baroness (1930/2). In the hospital at Heerlen she had to consent to serve as a study object for midwives (1930/5).

On February 9, 1931 Thomas Bernhard was born in Heerlen. Hertha Bernhard had asked the director of the

Now she fled from the site of her disgrace to the Netherlands where she found refuge with the aforementioned friend in Rotterdam. A short while later she gave birth to a son in a convent in Heerlen, which also specialized in taking care of so-called fallen girls. Right after birth, as I can see in a photograph, I had more hair than I have ever seen before on the head of a newborn. I am said to have been a cheerful child, and my mother, like all mothers, a happy one. (Ki 58)

She knew that she had borne an extraordinary child, but one with dreadful consequences. (Ki 50)

In 1931, when I was born, the place of my birth was not by accident Heerlen in the Netherlands, where my mother, following the advice of a friend working there, had fled right at that moment when I decided to come finally into this world, calling for a quick birth. In Henndorf my birth would have been completely impossible, a scandal, and the damnation of my mother would have been the inevitable consequence at a time when nobody wanted illegitimate children. (Ki 56/57)

hospital in Heerlen to accept her son in his second institution in Amsterdam, but Dr. Mülemann could not help.

In Rotterdam Hertha Bernhard stayed at Piersonstraat 19/3. Since she was unable to find a place in a nursery for the child, she gave him, only a few weeks after birth, to a home in Westeinde, Watergenstraat 107. They were a poor fisherman's family living "in an old street with peculiar-looking buildings" (Ud/29). Thomas Bernhard stayed there until Pentecost in 1931.

After Hertha Bernhard had given birth, her parents in Vienna were highly concerned because she did not have a place to work in Rotterdam. She herself was worried as well: "I know how you feel and therefore it is too painful for me to wait and wait without any money coming in. I do not have any advice, nor solution . . ." (Ud/27).

At Pentecost of 1931 she sent Thomas Bernhard to Hilgesheim because his surroundings were cleaner there. Hilgesheim was half an hour away from Rotterdam.

During this time she came to the conclusion to leave the child with her parents in Vienna. Since employment opportunities were better in the Netherlands, Hertha would stay there for the time being until "the most essential things are acquired at home" (Ud/29). Anna Bernhard, who had had to work out of town since February 1930, was able to stay at home and take care of her grandchild.

In July 1932 Thomas Bernhard was with his grandparents in Vienna (1932/2).

In 1935 Hertha Bernhard returned to Vienna where she met Emil Fabjan (born September 24, 1913).

The opportunity to leave me in the convent in Heerlen had been only of short duration; my mother had to collect me; she traveled to Rotterdam carrying me in a small laundry basket borrowed from her friend. Since she could not earn her living and be with me at the same time, she had to give me away. The solution was a trawler docking in the harbor of Rotterdam, where the trawler owner's wife fostered children below deck; seven to eight newborns were hanging in hammocks from the wooden ceiling, and as requested they were lowered and shown to the mothers coming by once or twice a week. I was said to have cried miserably and my face was covered with boils and from the hammocks came an incredible stench and impenetrable fumes. But my mother had no choice. She visited me, as I know, on Sundays, for during the week she worked as a maid to support herself and to pay the fees for my accommodation on the ship. (Ki 58/59)

From now on, I did not only have a mother, I had grandparents. In the Wernhardstraße in the 16th district, close to the Wilhelminenspital I uttered the word "grandfather" for the first time in my life. (Ki 61)

SEEKIRCHEN

At the beginning of 1935 Johannes Freumbichler, Anna Bernhard, and their grandchild Thomas moved to Seekirchen. Hertha Bernhard and Emil Fabjan stayed in Vienna. Freumbichler trusted Emil Fabjan: "Our correspondence will get started despite all the obstacles and will then, as I hope, go on to last until the end of our lives" (Fab/Fr 1935/1).

Farald lived with his parents in Seekirchen. In 1927 he had begun a second apprenticeship in Graz to become a sign painter; however, to his father's disappointment he had abandoned it without a certificate (1929/16).

Because the flat in Seekirchen was very damp, the Freumbichler family rented a "dry, wooden house in lofty heights" from a farmer named Mirtlbauer in June 1935 (Fab/Fr 1935/1). "The new home has, of course, because of its primitiveness, many flaws, but its advantages, at least seen from our viewpoint, are worth three times more. It is surrounded completely by wheat fields and lush meadows with a truly lovely view of Seekirchen. No noise, no dust, no vermin, no people. Everything that I have been longing for so desperately is right here," Freumbichler wrote to Emil Fabjan on June 24, 1935 (ibid.).

After the move Freumbichler had to comply with his previously established principles: "To get things in order, begin a new work and strive for laurels" (ibid.).

A few steps away from the wooden cabin was an inn, the "Bräukeller," an "old historic farmers' brew joint, where my father used to sit telling me about it, when I was a child" (Fab/Fr 1935/2). Its atmosphere inspired Freumbichler to a book "full of haunt, ghosts and human truth and foolishness" (Fab/Fr 1935/3). The novel could

They must have considered the Vienna of that time as hell in which everything was at stake every day. From this hell my grandfather wanted to get out as fast as possible, even if it meant paying the price of returning to where he had fled from thirty years earlier. After all, he had been working in these thirty years, even if he remained a total failure. (Ki 66)

My grandfather had finally turned his back on Vienna; later he wondered how he could have had the strength to do so. The departure from Vienna to the countryside, only six kilometers from Henndorf, which means further away from the immediate home, must have been carried out rather hastily, for I remember that our first stop was at the inn of the railway station in Seekirchen. For several weeks we lived in a guest room, with our laundry constantly hanging over our heads, and when I said good-night—at that time I would still fold my hands—I looked through a tall window directly onto the lake getting darker under the setting sun. Except for thousands of books which were to come later, we had taken along nothing from Vienna, neither furniture nor anything else, only two suitcases and our clothes. (Ki 67)

He had suffered from a lung disease once, this may have determined his decision to leave Vienna and go to Seekirchen. (Ki 81)

be completed quickly "since I have a similar book in front of me, written over fifteen years ago" (Fab/Fr 1935/3). He saw the "inhabitants of a village on piles" as the characters of the novel: "A couple of thousand years ago this place was probably a real pile village, and there are many figures and events that entice me to write such a novel, somehow in the style of Th. V. Vischer. The farmer whom we rented our lodging from is a character who will be perfectly suitable for this purpose" (Fab/Fr 1935/1).

Johannes Freumbichler was quite lonely in Wimm, as the area around Seekirchen is called. He missed the Vienna forests, the vineyards, "the almost southern sunlight, the wonderful walks and a few amiable, beloved persons" (Fab/Fr 1935/2). The reason for this loneliness was that in his new environment he did not possess the most important thing: "The ability to concentrate on intellectual work" (Fab/Fr 1935/2). However, he knew the key to success: *patience*.

Constantly he recalled his idol's mottoes in order to reinforce his demands on himself. In Goethe's works he read: "Impatience creates impatience tenfold, one assumes one is getting closer to the goal, but one only gets further away" (Fab/Fr 1935/3). Or: "There is no greater artist than continuous work; only God can create at once, human endeavors grow step by step" (ibid.). A saying by Govineau had eternal validity: "Art is the only virtue, the only truth, the only happiness" (ibid.). Freumbichler also forced himself to "work incessantly on improving and refining his inner self, on his teaching, his education" (Fab/Fr 1936/2).

His isolation in writing, his exclusion from the artistic world, gave rise to his wish to revive the potential artist

One day the three of us, my grandfather, my grand-mother and I, pulled an old, small cart, probably ac-quired not only for this purpose, packed with all our belongings to the so-called "Bräuhaushöhe." In front of the old "Bräuhaus," a three-hundred-year-old building left to decay, which housed beer and wine in its huge cellars and in which, as my grandfather said, some des-parately poor people lived for a ridiculously low fee, there stood a small one-story wooden house overlooking the marketplace of Seekirchen. It had been built from railway sleepers and belonged to a farmer living near the "Hippinghof." It was a cheerful sight with its large balcony on the front. From this balcony one could see the lake beyond the market and, on clear days, the mountains. It was one of the cheapest accommodations in the whole area. We had a fantastic view, and there was a garden under the balcony; there were two rooms downstairs and two upstairs and a spacious staircase with a door onto the balcony. (Ki 74/75)

On the ground floor we had one large room which was accessible to everybody. Next to it was grandfather's study, which I was not allowed to enter unless explicitly told to. (Ki 76)

. . . in the so-called "Mirtelbauernhäusl," named after its owner, was a huge realm in which the sun would never set. (Ki 84)

. . . I had read Hunger *by Hamsun,* Raw Youth *by Dos-toevsky and* Elective Affinities *by Goethe and had made notes like my grandfather used to all his life. (A 151/152)*

108

in people whom he loved. He wanted to get Emil Fabjan, who did wood carvings, to continue his craft as an
art: "Now that the evenings get longer, go and resume
your practical work with your wood carving and do not
give up until you perfectly master the technique. The
money must not concern you. For I hope and expect and
will not rest before you decide to zealously continue
with your idea of being an artist, a wood carver. Other
people may say what they want" (Fab/Fr 1935/2). His
continuous efforts to realize his plans would serve as an
example to others. "My first useful works, small narratives, were printed in 1916, in the middle of the World
War, and now, after twenty years I am not able to find
a publisher for my works to generate some revenue.
Lately, since the summer of 1934, I have been utterly
disappointed by these failures, . . . However, I was able
to recover from this misery, and I have been working on
new projects" (Fab/Fr 1935/3).

Freumbichler wrote this letter to Fabjan in October
1935. At this time he worked on a novel titled *Io ti
vedo*, which was expected to comprise about a thousand
pages and which was set among the Indians of Brazil.
His idol was Karl May. He reported that work was
progressing well: "I am not running out of ideas. All I
have to do, without particular concern or physical pain,
is to sit down, and my imagination takes off all by itself" (ibid.).

In 1935 Freumbichler managed to publish a narrative
with a calendar publisher (Fab/Fr 1935/2).

At the same time, in the fall of 1935, Anna Bernhard
wrote to Carl Zuckmayer. Since 1933 Zuckmayer and
his wife Alice had been living in Henndorf in the
"Wiesmühle" (their residence in Vienna was at Vienna
VIII, Mentergasse 11). Anna Bernhard sent him one of

These and other statements I have often heard from my grandfather, the writer, without understanding them, while accompanying him on his walks; he loved Montaigne and I share this love with him. (U 127)

. . . and I had only demanded that my family forward those books—from my grandfather's bookcase to Groß-gmain—which I know had been of profound importance to my grandfather and which I assumed to be able to understand. In such a way I had become familiar with the most important works of Shakespeare and Stifter, Lenau and Cervantes without being able to say today that I fully understood the whole encompassing richness of this literature, but I have absorbed them with grateful-ness and the willingness to comprehend and I profited from that. I had read Montaigne, Pascal, and Peguy, the philosophers who would later always accompany me and who have always been important to me. And, of course, Schopenhauer, into whose world and mind, naturally not his philosophy, I had been introduced by my grandfather. (A 140/141)

His situation was the worst that one could imagine, but he fought, he still fought after four decades of downright failure, where others would have given up long ago. He had not given up. With the growing unbearable failures his obsession for this subject which was his work, grew stronger. (Ke 100)

Johannes Freumbichler's novels secretly. Zuckmayer: "Maybe I can help you somehow" (Zuck 1935/1). Only in July 1936 did Zuckmayer finally read *Philomena Ellenhub*, which had been rejected by the publishers Speidel, Pustet and Herder. But Freumbichler was convinced: "I certainly do not possess any magic, but my *Philomena Ellenhub* does" (Fab/Fr 1936/1). Zuckmayer's impression while reading it: "Let me tell you right away that it is extremely captivating, and already now I have the feeling it is an unusual, beautiful piece of work and I sense a strong and unique poetic personality, to commit myself to which will be a pleasure and a duty!" (Zuck 1936/1). Zuckmayer wanted to express this conviction "right before the public" (ibid.). His wife Alice assisted him by editing the first and second versions: "Up to now I have compared fifty pages sentence for sentence and transferred into the first version small, and as my husband thinks, very good ideas from the second one. I also marked for him the places—whole paragraphs—which you wanted to omit in the second version—he was shocked to see what you wanted to do, and in his opinion it is to be blamed on the publishers who wanted you to forge your novel into another Ganghofer (Zuck 1936/4).

With loving affection I watched him write, my grand-mother getting out of his way; quietly she served break-fast, lunch, supper; being quiet so as not to disturb my grandfather became the main discipline, as long as he lived quiet was our highest duty. Every word had to be spoken in a low voice, we had to walk on tiptoes, we had to act constantly in a quiet manner. The head is as fragile as an egg, my grandfather used to say. It made sense to me and at the same time it shocked me. He got up at three in the morning, at nine he would go for a walk. In the afternoon he would work for two hours be-tween three and five. (Ki 71/72)

All hope was now concentrated not on Traunstein, but on a famous writer living close by in his hometown of Henndorf. It was said that my grandmother had taken a manuscript to the well-known man, who was trying to find a publisher to have it printed. We waited. The walks were no longer a relief, they were a torture. My grand-father began threatening to commit suicide again. (Ki 98)

Famous actors, writers, sculptors, indeed any kind of artists or scholars imaginable were visiting the so-called "Wiesmühle." The famous writer was so different from my grandfather who was also a writer, but not a famous one. (Ki 102)

Carl Zuckmayer sent the revised work to Hermann Hesse, Gerhart Hauptmann and Thomas Mann (Zuck 1936/4).

One copy went to Paul Zsolnay, who accepted *Philomena Ellenhub*. Freumbichler wrote to Alice Zuckmayer: "September 1936 will be the most important chapter in the annals of my life" (Zuck 1936/6).

A literary success could make it possible to fulfill an old personal wish for Johannes Freumbichler and Anna Bernhard: their marriage. They had been living together for thirty-two years. On June 16, 1936 Freumbichler wrote to his companion: "As far as our wedding is concerned, we will have to postpone it if my failures appear at such regular intervals. However, we are short 100 Schilling for our wedding" (Fab/Fr 1936/5).

In fall of 1936 Emil Fabjan and Hertha Bernhard were married in Seekirchen. For the foreseeable future they stayed in Vienna (Fab/Fr 1936/8).

In October 1936 Freumbichler corrected the proofs of *Philomena Ellenhub* (Fab/Fr 1936/8). In February 1937 he expressed his worries: "will it be sold???!!!" (Fab/Fr 1937/1). He was in a depressed mood "particularly with a view to the fact that we are getting older and are basically without an income" (ibid.).

Freumbichler had waited for three years to see his novel published, "in bitter sorrow" and "often in complete despair" (ibid.). After the printing of *Mena* Freumbichler continued with the first version of *Atahuala, das Land der weiβen Indianer* (Atahuala, Land of White Indians); such was the new title for *Io ti vedo*. He wanted to have the book printed by fall 1938. In February 1937 he wrote: ". . . and I do not want to stop until it is finished. One of these books has to save

113

One day a telegram arrived informing my grandfather that his novel had been accepted. By a publisher in Vienna. The famous man had kept his promise, the book was published and my grandfather received a national prize for it. (Ki 100)

. . . more than with my mother I had spent time with my grandparents, for it was there that I always received affection and understanding and sympathy, and the kind of love that I could not find anywhere else, and I had grown up under the protection and with the unnoticed education given to me by my grandfather. My fondest memories were the walks together with my grandfather, the wanderings for hours through nature and the observations made throughout these strolls, observations he developed in me to an art of observation. Attentive to everything which was pointed out to me by my grandfather, I may say that the time with my grandfather was the only useful school and decisive for my whole later life, for it was he and nobody else who taught me what life was about and who brought me into touch with life by first bringing me into touch with nature. All my knowledge I owe to this human being who had the most profound influence on my life and existence. (U 129)

My grandfather had literally withdrawn me from their educational influence from the very beginning of my life and had sheltered me entirely with his protection and his intellect. They had no opportunity of influencing me during these eighteen years. My grandfather had excluded them from my education. (A 109/110)

us from poverty" (Fab/Fr 1937/1). Meanwhile he had completed twenty rural stories in the hope "that Zsolnay will publish them this fall" (Fab/Fr 1937/1).

Just four weeks after *Philomena Ellenhub* had been published, one success was visible: "As far as I can judge this matter now and from my isolated hermit's view, it is reviewed in almost all newspapers in a supportive and partly even enthusiastic manner. In particular, the *Wiener Tagblatt* (*Vienna Daily*) dedicated a very remarkable article of six columns which I truly enjoyed. Even more did I like the news that Gerhart Hauptmann reads the novel and as it seems, not without showing a certain degree of appreciation" (Fab/Fr 1937/2).

With support from Carl Zuckmayer, Johannes Freumbichler was awarded the Austrian State Prize for Literature for *Philomena Ellenhub. A Salzburg Rural Novel.* The book is dedicated to his mother Maria Freumbichler.

The time that Johannes Freumbichler did not spend on writing he shared with his grandchild Thomas. Every day he took him along on his walks: "In the afternoon Thomas and I wander through meadows, fields and forests. Everything is filled with the birds' songs. As if all life were merely play and dance. Well, in one's youth it is only play and dance. Thomas picks huge bouquets of wild flowers and he proves to be a master in spotting genuine violets" (Fab/Fr 1936/2).

Grandfather and grandchild appeared as kindred spirits: ". . . it is still the time of the frosty snowmen and we have to put up with these gentlemen. As soon as the sun comes out, Thomas and I will stroll in the afternoon through the lush and wonderful world of May" (Fab/Fr 1936/3).

115

But when I was allowed to accompany him, I was the happiest person. During these walks I was never allowed to speak, a rule which was only rarely relaxed. When he had a question to ask or if I had one. He was the one who would explain, the first and most important one to do this, actually the only one. With his walking stick he would point to animals and plants and give a little lecture on every animal and plant to which his stick drew attention. It is important to know what one sees. At least one has to be able, step by step, to describe things. One must know where it comes from, what it is. (Ki 80).

Quite naturally the difficult grandchild had, under the auspices of his grandfather, drifted away from them quite early spiritually and intellectually and had, corresponding to his character and always also to his age, pursued a critical view toward them, a fact which they could not bear over time and finally never accepted. For I had not grown up with them, but with my grandfather; I owed to him everything that made me ready for life and to a high degree always happy, not to them. (A 31/32)

At home as well Freumbichler took the child under his wing. Soon he discovered talents he deemed to be worth supporting. With pride he reported to his daughter Hertha: "His biggest passion at home is writing. These days he gets a few pennies and he disappears. What does he bring back from the store! A pen . . . And he can write the numbers one to ten in ink" (Fab/Fr 1936/2).

He found another artistic gift in Thomas: "Last night he showed us real theater—wearing a paper crown on his head and a long trailing cape—something he truly loves. On seeing this I thought he would have what it takes to be an actor. For he shows an intellectual swiftness which is amazing. One could, with a minimum of effort, make something special of him" (Fab/Fr 1936/4).

The grandfather also noticed a musical talent: "When I earn some money, the first thing I shall buy is a violin. If he starts now he will be an artist at twenty" (Fab/Fr 1936/4).

In fall 1936, Thomas Bernhard began his first year of school in Seekirchen. In October Freumbichler wrote: "Thomas Niklas is more than ambitious at school, and at home he cannot get enough of reading and writing until he is too tired in the evenings" (Fab/Fr 1936/7).

Carl Zuckmayer had also made an impression on the six-year-old Thomas Bernhard. When the Freumbichler family was invited to the Zuckmayer's home for Christmas Eve of 1936, Freumbichler had noted: "Thomas was seated to the left of Mr. Zuckmayer, the mother to the right. Thomas showed excellent table manners. Eight days later he described down to the last detail the events of the evening: 'Mr. Zuckmayer looked like a king from a fairytale book'" (Fab/Fr 1937/1).

It seemed that Freumbichler's love of his grandchild brought him peace. On a walk through Salzburg he felt

117

"Maybe it is the art of painting. You possess a great talent for drawing. Something artistic," he said. (Ki 154)

. . . but the hopelessness of teaching me the art of playing the violin became more and more obvious from lesson to lesson. Only for my grandfather, whom I loved, did I want to make progress in playing the violin, achieve something in the art of playing the violin, but the will to do this favor for my grandfather, to fulfill the wish of becoming a violin artist, was not enough in itself; every single lesson was the ultimate failure. (U 56)

I did not want to play the violin to begin with, I hated the instrument, but my grandfather saw the violinist in me. (Ki 159)

. . . the futility of teaching me the art of playing the violin. It had been my grandfather's wish to make an artist of me; the fact that I had been an artistic person had to lead him to try to make an artist of me and with all the love that also his grandchild extended to him all his life he had tried everything to make an artist out of me, make the artistic person into an artist, a musical artist. (U 55/56)

He had planned something big for me and had constantly talked about it and not only to me, and now I had ended up as a sales clerk in a grocery store in the basement of the "Scherzhauserfeldsiedlung." (Ke 74)

"that there is no greater happiness on earth than a few harmonizing persons spending the short years they are given here in love and kindness and showing each other as much goodness as they can" (Fab/Fr 1936/4).

He had this inner peace in spite of still living in the same poverty. Now he was even able to take a humorous look at his situation. He wrote to Hertha: "I cannot keep a rather painful matter from you: I do not have any pants to wear! This is a terrible thing. As I am sure there are enough old pants lying in boxes and attics, exposed to roaches, pants which would be anxiously willing to cover the thin legs of a poor poet" (Fab/Fr 1936/2). Emil Fabjan and Hertha helped by supplying clothes and food. Anna Bernhard found temporary work with a farmer named Hipping. Her remuneration was food (Fab/Fr 1936/6).

In October 1937, Emil Fabjan moved to Traunstein in Bavaria, where he stayed with the Poschinger family at Schaumburgergasse 4. Freumbichler had advised him against going to Seekirchen with Hertha because life there was too expensive. Like her father, Hertha suffered from a lung disease.

In January 1938 Hertha followed to Traunstein. With the new circumstances Freumbichler and his grandchild had to separate. Now Thomas Bernhard was supposed to live with his mother and the Vormund (guardian). This meant changing schools during the same month. Hertha wrote: "Wednesday was the big day, I went to the school with Thomas, what an amazement, the big beautiful school, these many children, the head of the school, a small hunchbacked man, was extremely friendly . . . for lunch Thomas came home with a boy from the neighborhood; but he was cheerful, for the teacher had told the other boys that Thomas spoke more articulately

Towards noon I would spot my grandfather in the distance and run to him across the fields. In summer he would wear only linen clothing and a Panama hat. He never walked without his stick. We understood each other. (Ki 79)

My grandfather, whom I loved more than anything else, suddenly became the well-dressed gentleman with his walking stick, whom people would watch curiously and at the same time suspiciously. A novelist, a thinker! The contempt he attracted was greater than the admiration. The gentleman could not even afford to buy a meal at the inn. Others went to work, he went for walks. My grandmother found work at the "Hippinggut," high above Seekirchen, she looked after the children and helped with the laundry. Everything she did she did with rigor, and soon she made friends. She earned enough that we could live on it. Her art of sewing, which had always been admired by everyone, could unfold to its entire beauty at the "Hippinggut." After a short time she was so popular that even the writer, the walker, the thinker profited from it. (Ki 69)

It made me unhappy that I was to move to Traunstein together with my mother and her husband even before my grandparents, whose move had not even been considered yet. One could not make me comprehend that life in Seekirchen was at an end. Again it had only been another intermediate stop. To live without my grandfather under the regime of a stranger staying with my mother who, depending on my grandfather's mood, was called alternately either "your father" or "your guardian," seemed to me the most incredible thing in the world. This catastrophe meant saying farewell to everything which had truly made my paradise. (Ki 96)

120

than all the others together, for some of them had ridiculed him for his pronunciation; on the first night Thomas said: 'I would rather go back to grandmother, I would not make any noise so that grandfather doesn't complain'" (Fab/Fr 1938/1).

On April 15, 1938 Hertha gave birth to her second son, Hans Peter.

In the fall of 1938 Zsolnay published the *Geschichten aus dem Salzburgischen* (Tales from Salzburg) and *Atahuala* with another revised title: *Atahuala oder die Suche nach einem Verschollenen* (Atahuala or the Search for a Lost One). On February 25, 1939 Freumbichler answered Alice Zuckmayer's question on the response to *Atahuala*: ". . . in my total isolation I haven't heard one single word about it" (Fab/Fr 1939/2).

Farald, who since 1936 had lived in Salzburg with his wife Fanny, typed his father's manuscripts into fair copy and also took care of his correspondence with publishers (Fab/Fr 1938/3).

In November 1938, after thirty-four years of having lived together, Johannes Freumbichler and Anna Bernhard got married. In Seekirchen they established a peaceful existence for themselves despite numerous deprivations. They would spend the evenings with reading, e.g., Goethe's *Dichtung und Wahrheit*: ". . . Mom reads and I listen, smoking my pipe . . . Reading together stimulates a lot, soothes one's nerves and lets you slip from the noisy daily business into a quiet dreamless night" (Fab/Fr 1939/1).

Apart from Goethe, Freumbichler read among others Schopenhauer, Nietzsche, Kant, Epictetus, Montaigne and Dchung-Dsi's *The True Book of the Southern Land of Blossoms*, a volume of Zen-Koans with commentary.

The peaceful life was disturbed. The Mirtlbauer

His son-in-law had found work in Bavaria, or better Germany, nowhere else. The paradise was lost. (Ki 95)

When I thought of Seekirchen I trembled with crying. I cried loudly when I was sure that nobody could hear me. (Ki 114)

I wished for only one thing in the world: that my grandfather would come and rescue me before it was too late. (Ki 115)

My grandfather and I went for long walks, already under the prospect of a final farewell to Seekirchen and the area around the Wallersee. I had already reached a certain level of maturity side by side with the philosopher and, in fact, being for my age educated above average without tumbling into a stage of life-threatening megalomania, my grandfather continued to introduce me to nature's peculiarities and boldnesses and corruptions and monstrosities. He had always been my teacher. (Ki 105/106)

wanted to bequeath his estate and use the wooden cabin for himself. This meant another change of residence. Freumbichler played with the idea of moving either to Neumarkt or Traunstein.

In Traunstein, Fabjan tried to find a "small flat." Traunstein held, of course, another treasure for Freumbichler: his grandchild.

TRAUNSTEIN

In the spring of 1939, Johannes Freumbichler and his wife moved to Ettendorf near Traunstein. By Christmas of the same year Freumbichler finished a volume with six narratives "which seem to me the best I have ever written" (Zuck 1939/2). With *Philomena Ellenhub's* success Freumbichler gained contact with other colleagues. Georg Schwarz, whom Freumbichler had known since 1941, referred him to Hermann Leins of the Wunderlich publishing house (1941/5).

In 1942 two of Freumbichler's works were published by Wunderlich: *Die Reise nach Waldprechting* (The Journey to Waldprechting) and the novel *Auszug und Heimkehr des Jodok Fink. Ein Buch vom Abenteuer des Lebens* (Departure and Return of Jodok Fink. A Book on the Adventure of Life).

In the fall of 1943, the Piper publishing house showed interest in *I Am Alone*, thoroughly supported by Schwarz. Schwarz thought: ". . . only the title would have to be changed" (1943/4). Freumbichler sent the manuscript also to the publisher Eugen Haendle.

In the fall of 1945, Schwarz again probed the possibilities with Hermann Leins for Freumbichler: "Yes-

A truck with books and manuscripts stopped in front of the house, the shelves were filled. From his early years on, since Basel, as he always said, my grandfather had collected books; they had no money, but always more books. Thousands. They did not have enough space in the study in the Mirtlbauernhäusl, and so they were stored in the attic. Now the walls of the new study in Ettendorf were lined with books. "I did not know that I had accumulated so much intellectual wealth," he said, "and so much nonsense." Hegel, Kant, Schopenhauer, these names were familiar to me, hiding something monstrous from me. "And then comes Shakespeare," my grandfather said. (Ki 116)

terday the owner of the R. Wunderlich Publishing Company of Tübingen was here. He liked the beginnings and endings of your narratives so much that he immediately took the manuscript to Tübingen. I think you could not hope for anything better" (1945/3).

During the years in Traunstein Freumbichler corresponded with Mrs. Agathe Wibe (born 1871) from Mosjgen in Norway. Farald had met her when he had been based there as a soldier during the Second World War. Mrs. Wibe was a woman of literary education. In *Philomena Ellenhub* she recognized influences of Selma Lagerlöf and in *Jodok Fink* the basis of Tolstoy's *Resurrection* (1942/10). She sent poems of Rilke to him. Her letters were an enrichment to Freumbichler: "When I recall the contents of your letters, which represent a literary treasure to me, I know that you are one of God's true children," he writes to her in 1948 (1948/2).

In the fall of 1945, Johannes and Anna Freumbichler were evicted from Traunstein. Emil Fabjan and his family also planned to leave Bavaria.

Anna Freumbichler thought of moving to Salzburg with her husband: "We have always hated the Hitler regime and we suffer innocently" (Zuck 1946/1). She had heard an impressive speech given by the Austrian president, Dr. Renner, in which he had said: "I have noticed with pleasure that gradually all the artists living abroad such as sculptors, painters, famous writers again look to their Austrian home and return in order to let the Austrian people enjoy their creations" (AB-JF/20). She urged upon Freumbichler that "your life's work is not completed yet" (ibid.). She asked Farald to visit the mayor's office in Salzburg to obtain support from the housing department: "Farald must take along the certifi-

125

Unfortunately his son-in-law, my guardian, had been able to find employment only here and so we were forced to exist in this abominable atmosphere. Now he himself was in Ettendorf, he said, but if he had to live over there, in Traunstein, no, then he would rather commit suicide. This is how he talked on his walks. (Ki 29)

. . . and of my uncle, who as a soldier had been based in Norway, and whom I remember as an ingenious communist and inventor that he had been all his life, a mind confronting me indeed with extraordinary and dangerous thoughts and incredible and equally dangerous ideas and a creative person, although seriously instable. (U 28)

cate of the Literary State Prize and the beautiful picture I have of you and ask for an appropriate villa apartment with 2 1/2 rooms close to the city" (ibid.).

In June 1946, having shared forty-two years with him, she wrote to Freumbichler: "You gave me a new life and I went through your school. These were hard years and heavy loads barred our way . . . May God let me accompany you for yet a short while, then I shall and want to be grateful . . . living by your side I have enjoyed all the happiness a woman can hope for" (AB-JF/21).

SALZBURG

Around mid-1946 Anna and Johannes Freumbichler returned to Salzburg. They shared living quarters with the Fabjan family and Farald, who had been divorced at the beginning of 1946, at Radetzkystraße 10.

Eight persons were crowded into just a few rooms. Only Freumbichler had a room of his own, for: "I must be alone to work" (Zuck 1946/3). However, Zsolnay was afraid that he would not be able to publish anything in the near future. Freumbichler had several manuscripts waiting. To make things worse, the income generated by *Jodok Fink* in Traunstein he had to leave behind because he had only been allowed to take 100 Reichsmark with him on leaving Germany (Zuck 1946/3).

In the spring of 1947, Wilhelm Niemeyer (born 1912), who wrote narratives and poems for journals (Nie 1947/1), contacted Johannes Freumbichler.

In 1947 Düsseldorf Druck Uerdingen printed the small volume of poems *Die lieben Gesellen* (The Dear Companions) and in 1948 *Der kleine Ring* (The Little Ring).

Being with him was comforting for me. As soon as I could I would run over the Taubenmarkt and the so-called Schnitzelbaumerstiege down to the gas works and on to Ettendorf. This took fifteen minutes. Panting I would fall into my grandfather's arms. (Ki 120)

. . . and in the afternoon up to the Holy Mountain to my grandfather. To stay overnight on the Holy Mountain meant the highest bliss for me. (Ki 125)

The house in which my grandparents had lived for several years belonged to a small farmer who owned six or seven cows and who worked his land with his wife, who walked bent over and who was almost totally mute and deaf. It was paradise to know my grandparents on a real farm, mind within matter so to speak. I loved the barn and the animals, I loved the smells, I loved the farmer couple. And this was reciprocated. No, it was not my imagination. I was allowed to watch when the cows were milked, I fed them, I cleaned them, I was there when they calved. I was there when the fields were ploughed, when the seed was planted and when the harvest was brought in. In winter I was allowed to spend time with them at home. There was no other place where I was happier. And here, where I was already so happy, my grandfather and grandmother lived too, which made my happiness complete. (Ki 28)

After having read *Jodok Fink* Niemeyer approached Dr. Haendle of the R. Wunderlich publishing house to obtain Freumbichler's address. Then he wrote on March 12, 1947: "I do not know anything of and about you except this book. I will always love it even if you do not return my greetings" (ibid.).

To him *Jodok Fink* was full of truth. On the novel's acceptance with the public he said: "The fact that you received only sparing recognition is no sign or judgment of the book, merely of the people who after reading it put it aside indifferently" (Nie 1947/2).

The contact between Niemeyer and Johannes Freumbichler did not last long, for in July Niemeyer, a former *Sturmführer* of the Hitler youth, was imprisoned (Nie 1947/3). On his release in March 1948 he received news of Freumbichler: The doctor had forbidden Freumbichler to write and to read because "little black devils" and "bewitched insects" danced before his eyes. Despite severe visual problems Freumbichler did not abandon his work. He worked on a collection of poems (about three hundred verses) titled *Erziehung zur Vernunft und Fröhlichkeit* (Education to Reason and Merriness); it was meant as a "call to youth" (Nie 1948/4). The narrative "Montbrison" had been finished in February 1948. Mrs. Johanna Hausl (Salzburg, Griesgasse 7) had typed the fair copy of the manuscript. A letter by Mrs. Hausl also reveals that one of Freumbichler's works titled "Ljubica" was ready for print. A publisher had not been found yet (1948/1).

In March 1948 Freumbichler worked on a novel, *Eling, das Tal der sieben Höfe* (Eling, Valley of the Seven Farms). About this project he wrote to Mrs. Agathe Wibe: "I am short of finishing a great novel— great in every respect, as I hope—many volumes type-

I myself hated Saturdays and Sundays, for on these days that I detested I was mercilessly confronted with the misery of my family; nine people living in three rooms getting on each other's nerves from dawn to dusk and, dependent on the meager income possibilities of my guardian and the cooking of my mother, suffered constant hunger and had nothing to wear. As I remember, they exchanged, for lack of clothing, shoes and vests and pants in order to be able to appear alternately as a decent human being. My grandfather alone had lived in the smallest of the rooms, but his room had been so small that he could hardly turn around; there he lived, shunned by his environment, with his books and his im-materialized ideas. Most of the time he would sit wrapped up in an old gray horse-blanket—in order to save what was left of the wood for the stove—at his desk without being actually able to work. I know he had locked himself up for days, and his wife, my grandmother, was waiting to hear the shot from the pistol that was lying on his desk—on his desk during the day and under his pillow by night. She was afraid of this shot. He had threatened her and all of us again and again with suicide. He had no money and hardly any strength left, he was starving like all of us. He knew nothing but hopelessness, two years after the war, in this bitter time. (Ke 92/93)

Johannes Freumbichler (ca. 1941)

. . . all they had left was their misery and the postwar catastrophe that had come down on them, without being able to cope with it. They were able only to stare at this catastrophe; continuously they stared at their own catastrophe that they called postwar catastrophe and did nothing. They were almost insane from staring at their catastrophe, their postwar catastrophe. (Ke 68)

To go with my grandfather, who was already very ill, up to the Mönchsberg—for hours if he had the strength for it which was only rarely now—this is what rescued me from Saturdays and Sundays. (Ke 95)

Once in a while I would go up the Mönchsberg alone and lie down in the grass and, sitting under a tree, write poems. (Ke 97)

The walks with him were nothing else but nature history, philosophy, mathematics, geometry, education, which made me happy. (Ki 82)

The adolescent, the grandchild of almost eighteen years, now had a much more intense—because above all intellectual—relationship with his grandfather than the boy who had sensed the bond only with his feelings. We did not have to exchange many words in order to understand each other and the rest. (A 34)

. . . so my grandfather. I was lucky enough to have the most loved person very close to me. (A 22)

written, and I am a bit proud that I endured, since 1943, despite all the misery and sorrow of the aerial bombs and that I have not deviated from my goal by a hair's breadth. One can only make something happen with fanatic dedication" (1948/2).

In 1948 *Philomena Ellenhub* was reprinted. Niemeyer received a copy. He remarked: ". . . It is with you, in and between the lines the prudence that always shines through" (Nie 1948/3). Freumbichler explained to him: "I have inherited the mastery of narrating. At our home we narrated quite a lot. What else was there to do on long winter nights?" According to Freumbichler, *Mena* was not a novel, more a chronicled account; "it possesses some vibrant vitality to refresh people who lead a tough life. What more rewarding thing is there for anyone" (Nie 1948/4).

In January 1949 Niemeyer received the last letter by Freumbichler: ". . . from your words one can see how difficult the past year was for you and how you still suffer from the one or other drudgery. Disease, sanatorium, stomach problems are not very nice words" (Nie 1949/1).

On February 11, 1949 Johnannes Freumbichler died in Salzburg.

On October 13, 1950 his daughter Hertha passed away.

In 1952 the poetry volume *Rosmarin und Nelken* (Rosemary and Cloves) by Johannes Freumbichler appeared posthumously in the Salzburger Druckerei publishing house. Alice Zuckmayer made efforts to publish *Eling* (Zuck 1949/1, 1950/1).

After her husband's death Anna Freumbichler lived in Salzburg-Gnigl, Mayerwiesweg 36. She died on July 1, 1965.

I admired my grandfather's toughness and the steady endurance and the tireless energy as he struggled with all his written and unwritten thoughts, because I admired everything about him; but at the same time I also saw this truly horrible insanity in which a man like my grandfather had to end up. (Ke 99)

All we heard was that he was working on his great novel, and my grandmother emphasized this statement, which was always made only in a low voice, with the words "it is to be over a thousand pages long." (Ki 117)

It was completely beyond my imagination how somebody could sit down and write a thousand pages. A hundred pages alone seemed incomprehensible to me. On the other hand, I can hear my grandfather say "everything one writes is nonsense." So how can he get the idea to write thousands of pages of nonsense? He always had the most incredible ideas, but he felt that he failed with these ideas. We all fail, he always said. This has been continuously my main thought. (Ki 117/118)

Johannes Freumbichler (ca. 1941)

Every day at three in the morning my grandfather made a fresh start; The Valley of the Seven Farms (Das Tal der sieben Höfe), a manuscript of 1,500 pages in three volumes, had made him for many years now take up the fight against death at three in the morning. Suffering all his life from a lung condition, he had made a habit of starting off his day at three in the morning, to start the deadly business of a fanatical writer and philosopher, wrapping himself in the horse-blanket and strapping an old belt around his waist. I could hear him take up the fight in his room at three in the morning, the fight against the impossible, against the complete hopelessness of writing. Lying in bed in the front room, right next to the door, with the attention of the sensitive and loving grandchild, not yet entirely familiar with all the cruel futilities and the hopelessness, I listened to the sounds, the repeated triumphs over the fatal fear and the newly challenged fight of despair of the human being whom I loved more than anyone else, the man who wanted to see his so-called main work complete. (Ke 98/99)

Out of respect for my grandfather, who worked for hours, everybody was as quiet as possible, and nobody would have dared to speak louder than necessary and make even the least irritating noise. All of us walked on tiptoes in order not to interrupt the progress of work on the Valley of the Seven Farms. (Ke 73)

136

I would like to complete this life portrait with one remark by Johannes Freumbichler. On February 1, 1927 he wrote to Anna Bernhard:

"You and your self were the solace and the treasure of my life" (1927/23).

In this circle of thoughts we achieve what we cannot achieve outside, the awareness of oneself and everything that is. (A 62)

I simply could not bear to see my grandfather go to the hospital. (A 30)

From time to time such diseases, real or not, as he expressed himself, were necessary to think these thoughts which one would not think of without such temporary illnesses. If we are not forced quite naturally to enter such areas of thoughts, which doubtless such hospitals and as a matter of fact hospitals in general are, we must go to such hospitals in an artificial way. (A 59)

In one of these barracks, as he told me, my grandfather was established. Now he had been in the hospital for over a week and the examinations he had gone through during this time had not yielded any results. Possibly the whole thing, according to him, was a false alarm, and he could go home soon. He did not feel ill at all. Most likely the doctor's suspicion was unfounded. According to him, he had to stay in the hospital only a few more days. (A 53/54)

I had never been able to imagine a life without him. (A27)

Johannes Freumbichler (1941)

By the time the doctors found out what kind of disease it was it was too late for a cure. The suspicion of the internist who had admitted him to the hospital had been confirmed by the examinations my grandfather had to undergo in the hospital. He should have been operated on six months earlier. At the time he was in the hospital his whole body, contrary to his claims, had been poisoned, and he did not die following an operation, as I had believed for several days, but from the sudden and complete breakdown and contamination of his blood. He had been conscious, according to my guardian, to the last moment. He only suffered from pain for a short while. The time of death was about six in the morning, a moment when he had been alone in the room with my grandmother. (A 101/102)

I had given my grandfather to understand what it meant to me to lie in his room and to look at the things in this room. He would bring me home and read to me from those books in his room, which I loved. We had agreed on that. He would go for longer and more frequent walks up the Mönchsberg than before, up to the Kapuzinerberg, which he loved, out to Hellbrunn in the Salzach meadows. (A 57)

Johannes Freumbichler with his grandson Thomas Bernhard (4 August 1943)

My grandmother had been a brave woman, and she was the only one of us who truly enjoyed her life, a life which ended rather miserably in a huge room crowded with thirty or more rusty iron beds in the Salzburg psychiatric hospital. I saw her a few days before her death, among the insane and crazy and utterly helpless and dying old people, hearing, but not understanding what I said. She was crying incessantly, and this last visit with my grandmother is probably the most painful memory of all. (U 133/134)

My grandfather's school that I had attended since infancy had ended with his death. He had released me from his lessons by being dead all of a sudden. It had been a basic school, finally a high school. Now I had, so I felt, a foundation on which to build my future. I could not have had a better foundation. (A 106/107)

We should get ready for a fresh start, a new start in life. My grandfather had talked about a future (for both of us), more important and more beautiful than the past. It was only a matter of wanting this future, both of us had the power to reach for it. The body obeys the mind and not the other way around. (A 34/35)

Johannes Freumbichler (ca. 1941)

. . . for ten days my grandfather had been lying out in the Maxglan graveyard, but the priest of Maxglan would not allow his burial because my grandfather had not been married in church; the widow, my grandmother, had tried everything to achieve the burial at the Maxglan grave- yard, where my grandfather should be buried, but this burial in the Maxglan graveyard, where my grandfather wished to be buried, was not granted. And no other graveyard, except the communal graveyard, which my grandfather detested, would take him . . . , for my grandmother and her son went to all the graveyards to get permission for the burial, but my grandfather was not accepted at any of the graveyards because he had not been married in church. And this in the year 1949! Only when my uncle, his son, went to the archbishop and told him that he would put the decaying corpse of his father, my grandfather, because he did not know what to do with it, he would put it in front of his palace door, did the archbishop give permission to have my grandfather buried at the Maxglan graveyard. I myself did not attend this burial, probably one of the saddest funerals in this town and carried out, as I know with all kinds of embar- rassments, because I had contracted a bad lung disease and was in the hospital. Today the grave of my grand- father is a so-called grave of honor. (U 60/62)

Twenty years of Vienna were therefore an incredible experience for my family because they had constantly been on the move and had changed their address around a hundred times, as I know. (Ki 68)

144

Addresses of Johannes Freumbichler from 1895 to 1949

November 1901 to January 1902: Salzburg, Gstättengasse, Stieglbräukeller

February 1902 to March 1902: Salzburg, Späthgasse 8/1

April 1902 to mid-March 1903: Altenburg, Karlstraße 6/2 (Saxony)

Mid-March 1903 to June 1903: Ilmenau, Alexanderstraße 23 (Thuringia)

July and August 1903: Ilmenau, Am Zeihenhaus 9/1 (Thuringia)

September 1903 to December 1903: Ilmenau, Marienstraße 14/2 (Thuringia)

January 1904 to April 1904: Basel, Hegenheimerstraße 12/2

May 1904 to fall 1905: Basel, Gasstraße 33/3

Fall 1905 to September 1906: Töll/Meran

October 1906 to mid-February 1907: Partschins/Meran

Mid-February 1907 to April 1907: Munich, Wolfratshauserstraße 31/3

May 1907 to May 1909: Meran, Lazag, Villa Rosenegg

June 1909 to August 1909: Meran, Obermais, Villa Lazag

September 1909 to April 1911: Henndorf/Wallersee and Munich

May 1911 to October 1911: Forstenried/Munich

November 1911 to mid-February 1912: Munich, Lindenschmidtstraße 29a/4

Mid-February to spring 1913: Munich, Implerstraße 67/4

Spring 1913: Bozen

Summer 1913: Henndorf

September 1913 to November 1914: Wien XIII, Barchettigasse 11/8

December 1914 to mid-February 1915: Wien III, Schanzgasse 21/2

Mid-February 1915 to mid-July 1916: Wien XIII, Flötzersteig 49/4

Mid-July 1916 to December 1934: Wien XVI, Wernhardstraße 6/3/13 (July and August: Kaiserleiten)

1935 to spring 1939: Seekirchen, Wimm (Bräukeller)

Spring 1939 to summer 1946: Traunstein, Ettendorf 5

Summer 1946 to February 1949: Salzburg, Radetzkystraße 10

Afterword

With this book Caroline Markolin has created a new literary-scholarly form: the *literary-biographical-comparative thriller*. Anyone who reads this as a derogatory term must be very musty, very "out," very averse to innovation. I am making this statement for Markolin's book full of admiration and in all seriousness. The Austrian publisher of the original, Otto Müller Verlag, immediately recognized the unusual qualities of the text, which fulfills the imperative of serious scholarly research and yet has every attribute to succeed in the larger commercial market. It features a lively, engaged style and presentation. Thus Markolin's study was not relegated to some scholarly series but appeared in the belletristic main program. The echo that the book received proved the decision right, and soon thereafter a French publisher followed with a translation. Now, finally, we can welcome the English version of this astounding work.

The importance of this biographical study on the Salzburg author Johannes Freumbichler (1881-1949), whose extremely productive life found little recognition despite occasional great moments of success, must be seen on several levels. We finally have in our hands a valid account of a writer who, given his obsession with the discipline of literary creation, was destined to become one of the great loners and outsiders of his era. Caroline Markolin, in writing this book, closes a gap in research and Germanistic knowledge that has been unjustified and

147

regrettable. Freumbichler's works are out of print, many of his texts were never published at all and are preserved in the Literary Archives of Salzburg, where Caroline Markolin once worked. In addition, Johannes Freumbichler is the grandfather of a world-famous author, namely, Thomas Bernhard. This fact, too, moves him into a special constellation deserving our interest. It is well known that Thomas Bernhard, this most negative and negating among recent German-language authors, always spoke of his writer-grandfather in terms of deepest love and highest admiration, truest gratitude and respect. There must be reason for this exception to Bernhard's almost permanent negative stance.

Caroline Markolin immediately felt the attraction and challenge to investigate the life of such a substantial, yet almost forgotten literary character as Freumbichler, and to compare her findings with the numerous references made to Freumbichler throughout the works of his grandson, Thomas Bernhard. The tragedy of Freumbichler's only marginally successful life becomes thus all the more obvious and moving when reflected in the most loving sentences of Bernhard's prose. Once the reading is completed, the reader discovers that he knows as much about Freumbichler as about Bernhard—and vice versa.

Caroline Markolin achieves this magical result, in the first place through the structure of her book. She chooses the folio format. The right-hand side of the book always contains information relating to Freumbichler's biography, the left-hand pages illustrates this with quotations from Bernhard's books, especially his four volumes of autobiographical text. As a result, the researcher's precision mirrors itself in literary conciseness, and our reading becomes an experience in breathless enthusiasm.

Caroline Markolin could not undertake such an enterprise without total distance and objectivity on her part. A difficult feat, to say the least, because it is love that dictates such a project and it can be felt everywhere. One need not remember the lukewarm clumsiness of many recent publications in literary criticism to feel grateful for this most unusual work of research and, yes, inspiration. Markolin's book does not have to shy away from comparison with scholarly work, yet it will be best read in a quiet hour in one's living room.

Finally I'd like to stress the state of shock and fond proximity to Freumbichler that the reader will develop while progressing through these pages. We learn about a poverty and an ability to deny oneself rarely told about in literary history. Freumbichler's own and his family's life were sacrificed, often with utmost egoism and brutality, to the obsession of writing. Success, if any, did not come until the author was in the sixth decade of his life. This biography stands out as the monument of a most unusual writer, but also as a memorial to those closest to him.

Let us mention Anna Bernhard as representative of others. After thirty-four years of togetherness in life she was to become Anna Freumbichler finally. Her leaving of a husband and two children in 1903 in order to live with the man and author she loved, was in her time an act of revolutionary courage. She then gave birth to two of his children, including, in 1904, Hertha, the future mother of Thomas Bernhard. Without Anna's total self-negation in order to help her lover and common-law husband, he would have never been able to pursue his art. It is her love—and Caroline Markolin's wonderful gift in describing it—that sets almost every page of this book ablaze. When in 1937, helped by Carl Zuckmayer, Johannes Freumbichler became a Zsolnay author and received the Austrian State Prize for his Novel *Philomena Ellenhub*, it was an award equally deserved by Anna.

Caroline Markolin's book is not just a brilliant literary study, it does more than satisfy the critical inquiring mind: it renders justice and destroys oblivion. I, for one, wish to thank her for this. Readers, I suspect, will all feel the same.

Erich Wolfgang Skwara

ARIADNE PRESS

Studies in Austrian Literature, Culture and Thought

*Major Figures of
Modern Austrian Literature*
Edited by
Donald G. Daviau

*Major Figures of
Turn-of-the-Century
Austrian Literature*
Edited by Donald G. Daviau

*Austrian Writers and the
Anschluss: Understanding the
Past—Overcoming the Past*
Edited by Donald G. Daviau

*Introducing Austria
A Short History*
By Lonnie Johnson

*Coexistent Contradictions
Joseph Roth in Retrospect*
Edited by
Helen Chambers

*The Verbal and Visual Art of
Alfred Kubin*
By Phillip H. Rhein

*Kafka and Language
In the Stream of
Thoughts and Life*
By G. von Natzmer Cooper

*Robert Musil and the Tradition
of the German Novelle*
By Kathleen O'Connor

*Austria in the Thirties
Culture and Politics*
Edited by Kenneth Segar
and John Warren

*Stefan Zweig:
An International Bibliography*
By Randolph J. Klawiter

*Austrian Foreign Policy
Yearbook*
Report of the Austrian Federal
Ministry for Foreign Affairs
for the Year 1990

*Quietude and Quest
Protagonists and Antagonists in
the Theater, on and off Stage
As Seen Through the Eyes of
Leon Askin*
Leon Askin and C. Melvin Davidson

*"What People Call Pessimism":
Sigmund Freud, Arthur Schnitzler
and Nineteenth-Century
Controversy at the University
of Vienna Medical School*
By Mark Luprecht

Arthur Schnitzler and Politics
By Adrian Clive Roberts

*Structures of Disintegration
Narrative Strategies in
Elias Canetti's* Die Blendung
By David Darby

ARIADNE PRESS

Translation Series:

February Shadows
By Elisabeth Reichart
Translated by Donna L. Hoffmeister
Afterword by Christa Wolf

Night Over Vienna
By Lili Körber
Translated by Viktoria Hertling
and Kay M. Stone. Commentary
by Viktoria Hertling

The Cool Million
By Erich Wolfgang Skwara
Translated by Harvey I. Dunkle
Preface by Martin Walser
Afterword by Richard Exner

Buried in the Sands of Time
Poetry by Janko Ferk
English/German/Slovenian
English Translation
by Herbert Kuhner

Puntigam or The Art of Forgetting
By Gerald Szyszkowitz
Translated by Adrian Del Caro
Preface by Simon Wiesenthal
Afterword by Jürgen Koppensteiner

Negatives of My Father
By Peter Henisch
Translated and with an Afterword
by Anne C. Ulmer

On the Other Side
By Gerald Szyszkowitz
Translated by Todd C. Hanlin
Afterword by Jürgen Koppensteiner

I Want to Speak
The Tragedy and Banality
of Survival in
Terezin and Auschwitz
By Margareta Glas-Larsson
Edited and with a Commentary
by Gerhard Botz
Translated by Lowell A. Bangerter

The Works of Solitude
By György Sebestyén
Translated and with an
Afterword by
Michael Mitchell

Remembering Gardens
By Kurt Klinger
Translated by Harvey I. Dunkle

Deserter
By Anton Fuchs
Translated and with an Afterword
by Todd C. Hanlin

From Here to There
By Peter Rosei
Translated and with an Afterword
by Kathleen Thorpe

The Angel of the West Window
By Gustav Meyrink
Translated by Michael Mitchell

Relationships
An Anthology of Contemporary
Austrian Literature
Selected and with an Introduction
by Adolf Opel